Fourth edition

Project

Workbook

with audio CD
and online practice

1

OXFORD

Tom Hutchinson
Janet Hardy-Gould

1 Introduction

1A Hello

Introductions

1 ✱ **Complete the bubbles.**

1. H _i_. M___ n___m___'s Adam Jackson. Wh___ ___'s y___ ___r n___m___?

2. H___ll___. M___ n___m___'s Danielle Smith.

3. H___. I'___ Lucas Owen.

4. H___ll___. I'___ Emma Scott. Wh___ ___'s y___ ___r n___m___?

2 ✱ **Find eight more names.**

Andy   Carla   Joe   ~~Mel~~   Mickey
Millie   Molly   Mut   Ravi

p	j	m	e	l	q	u	t	m	d
g	m	i	l	l	i	e	r	o	m
a	w	u	z	h	e	k	a	l	u
n	d	c	a	r	l	a	v	l	t
d	j	o	e	v	t	s	i	y	x
y	t	r	f	m	i	c	k	e	y

3 ★★ ▬ **Complete the dialogues. Put the words in the correct order.**

your   What's   name

Lucy   Hi, I'm Lucy. ¹ _What's your name_ ?

Jack   name's   My

Jack   ² _____ .

you   are   How

Will   Hi, Lucy. ³ _____ ?

thanks   fine   I'm   you   And

Lucy   ⁴ _____ . _____ ?

thanks   Fine

Will   ⁵ _____ .

See   later   you

Lucy   ⁶ _____ !

Bye   Yes

Jack and   ⁷ _____ . _____ !
Will

4 ★★ 🎧 1.2 **Listen. Complete the dialogue. Use the phrases in the box.**

And   See   you (x2)   Fine   thanks   ~~How~~

1 Hi, Anna.

2 Oh, hello, James! _How_ are _____ ?

3 I'm fine, _____ . _____ you?

4 _____ , thanks.

5 OK. _____ you later!

6 Bye, see _____ !

Writing

5 ★★★ **Complete the dialogue.**

Sam   H_ello, I'm Sam. What's your name_ ?

Nina   M_____ .

Sam   H_____ ! H_____ ?

Nina   F_____ .

Sam   O_____ !

Nina   B_____ !

1B In the classroom

Articles a / an

1 ✱ **Complete with a or an.**

1. _a_ boy
2. _____ door
3. _____ orange
4. _____ chair
5. _____ apple
6. _____ watch
7. _____ cat
8. _____ woman
9. _____ man
10. _____ umbrella

Vocabulary

2 ✱ **Write the missing letters.**

Across: 3

1
5
8

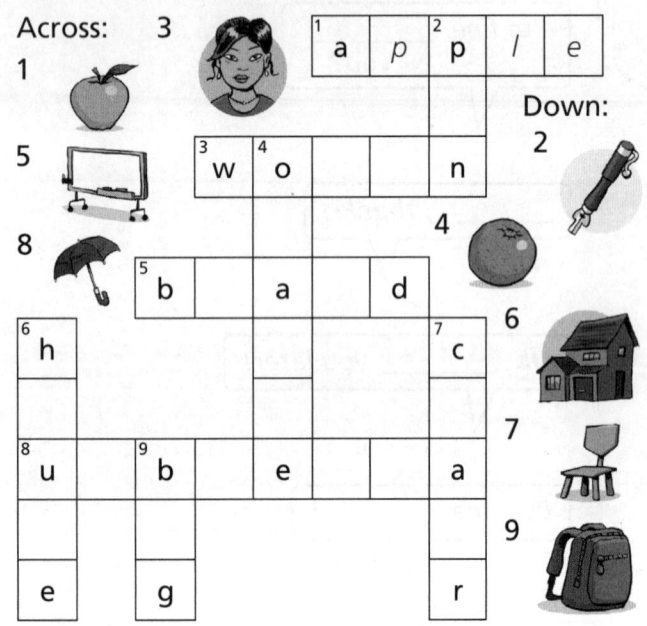

Down:
2
4
6
7
9

1 a	p	2 p	l	e

3 w	4 o		n

5 b	a	d

6 h			7 c

8 u	9 b	e	a

e	g		r

3 ✱✱ **Look at the picture. Write what you can see. Use a or an.**

1. _a picture_
2. _____
3. _____
4. _____
5. _____
6. _____
7. _____
8. _____

What's this? / It's …

4 ✱✱✱ **Complete the bubbles.**

1. What's t_____?   It's _a board._

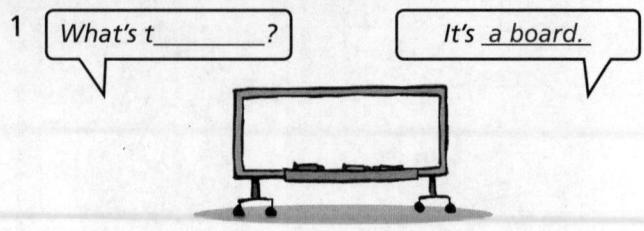

2. W_____
   t_____?

3.

4.

5.

6.

Listening

5 ✶✶ 🎧 1.3 **Listen and write the negative.**

1	*Don't stand up.*	5	
2		6	
3		7	
4		8	

Classroom instructions

6 ✶✶✶ **Write the instructions.**

1   *Listen.*

5 _____

2 _____ pencil.

6 _____

3 _____ exercise book.

7 _____

4 _____ picture.

8 _____

1C Numbers

Numbers

1 ✱ **Count and write the numbers.**

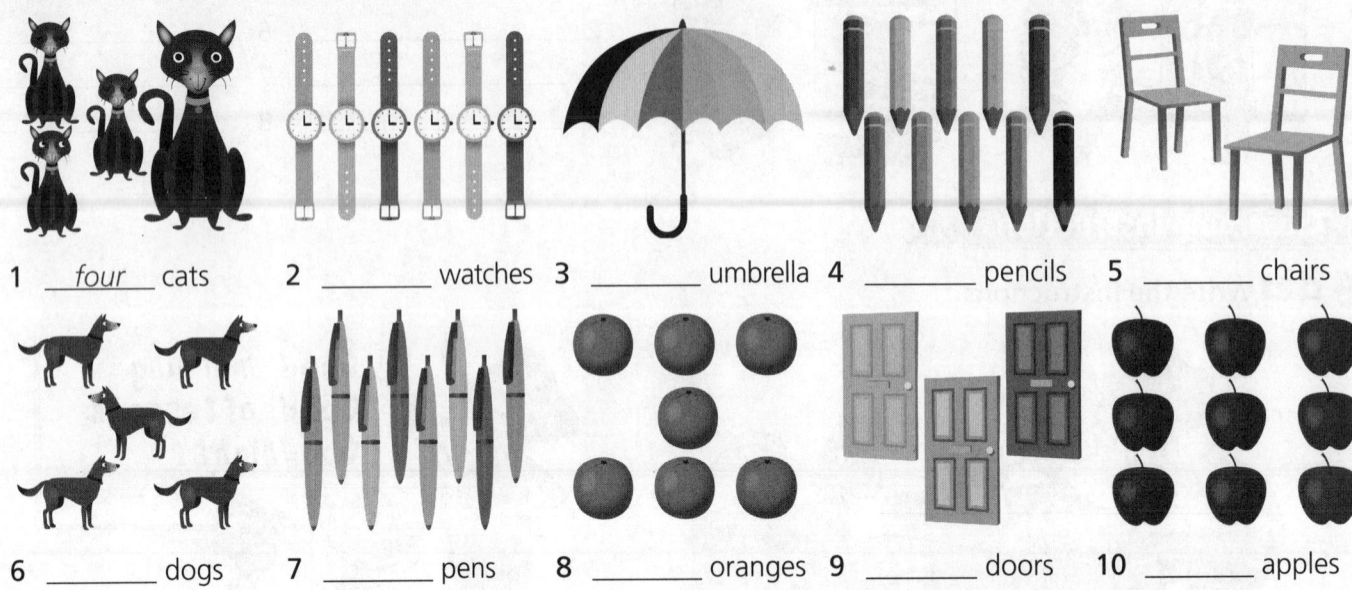

1 _four_ cats   2 _____ watches   3 _____ umbrella   4 _____ pencils   5 _____ chairs

6 _____ dogs   7 _____ pens   8 _____ oranges   9 _____ doors   10 _____ apples

2 ✱✱ **Match the people (1–6) to the phones (a–f).**

> My phone number is oh one two one, four nine six, oh five three.

> My phone number is oh two oh, seven nine four, six oh seven, six eight.

> My phone number is oh double seven, double oh nine, double oh one, three two.

1 Laura _b_   2 Ivan _____   3 Maryam _____

> My phone number is oh one three one, four nine six, oh three five.

> My phone number is oh two oh, seven nine four, six oh six, eight seven.

> My phone number is oh double seven, double oh nine, double oh two, three one.

4 Jacob _____   5 Eva _____   6 Ashraf _____

 a   07700 900132

 b   0121 496053

 c   02079 460687

 d   07700 900231

 e   0131 496035

 f   02079 460768

Listening

3 ✱✱ 🎧 1.4 **Listen and correct the numbers.**

1 What's your phone number?
It's 01632852749. __9__

2 What's your number?
My phone number's 01914980614. _____

3 What's your number?
It's 02890180586. _____

4 What's your mobile number?
My mobile number is 07700900433. _____

5 What's your phone number?
It's 02079460337. _____

6 What's your number?
My phone number's 01414906715. _____

4 ✱ Match the numbers to the words.

1 **67** ——— thirty-five

2 **93** fourteen

3 **9** fifty-six

4 **48** sixty-seven

5 **14** nine

6 **82** ninety-three

7 **35** forty-eight

8 **56** eighty-two

5 ✱✱ Write the numbers.

1 rehte _____ _three_

2 envse _____ _____

3 ewtvle _____ _____

4 hnigetee _____ _____

5 wynett-neo _____ _____

6 yhtrit _____ _____

7 tiffy-ifev _____ _____

8 innyte-wot _____ _____

6 ✱✱ Find the numbers.

twenty fifty-five eighty-six a hundred forty-three
twelve sixteen twenty-eight thirty-seven ten
sixty-one seventy-six eleven

2	0	3	2	5	5	9	9	4	0	4	0	7
5	3	7	9	1	1	1	0	0	8	5	7	2
1	9	1	2	3	0	4	3	2	6	3	9	1
1	7	0	2	3	4	6	9	2	5	9	8	5
5	8	1	4	7	4	7	3	2	5	3	0	1
3	0	9	5	6	9	4	5	9	4	9	9	4
6	3	6	1	7	2	9	8	2	6	0	1	3
6	4	0	8	0	1	0	8	6	5	2	3	9
3	8	3	4	4	5	7	7	6	4	4	7	2
5	2	5	1	6	7	2	8	4	1	3	5	1

7 ✱✱✱ Put the numbers and words in the correct order.

19 **37** FIFTEEN **4**
eleven SEVENTY-TWO
32 twenty **99** sixty
forty-one 50 16 26
80 77 a hundred
eighteen twenty-eight **13**
one **9** twelve 90

one, 4, _____

_____

_____

_____

1D How do you spell that?

The alphabet

1 ⭐ Write the missing letters.

a b _ d e _ _ **h i** _ **k** _ **m n** _ _ **q** r _ **t** _ v _ x _ **z**

2 ⭐⭐ Write the words.

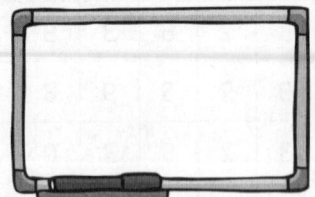   

1 abdro _____*board*_____   2 rlbaelum _____   3 thawc _____   4 orod _____

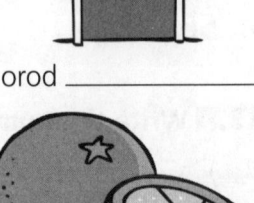 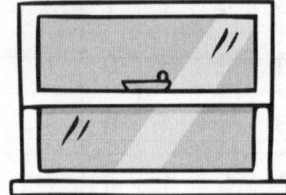  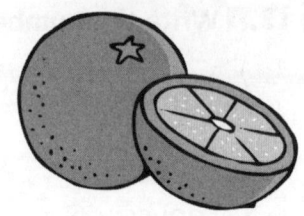

5 rihca _____   6 dnwowi _____   7 eusho _____   8 nregoa _____

Listening

3 ⭐⭐ 🎧 1.5 Listen and spell the names.

1 _A l i c i a_   2 _ _ _ _ _ _ _   3 _ _ _ _ _ _ _   4 _ _ _ _ _ _ _

5 _ _ _ _ _ _   6 _ _ _ _ _ _ _   7 _ _ _ _ _ _   8 _ _ _ _ _ _

Plurals

4 ⭐⭐ Label the pictures.

 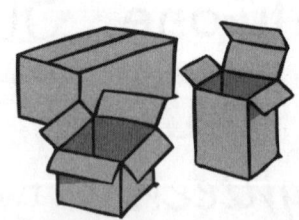  

1 _two girls_ _____   2 _____   3 _____   4 _____

5 _____   6 _____   7 _____   8 _____

There is / are

5 ** Look at the picture. Correct the sentences.

1 There's a dog.
   There's a cat.

2 There are two girls.

   _____

3 There's a mirror.

   _____

4 There are two oranges.

   _____

5 There's a woman.

   _____

6 There are three pens on the table.

   _____

7 There are two watches on the table.

   _____

8 There's a toothbrush on the chair.

   _____

6 *** Find six more differences between the pictures.

Picture A

1 *There's one desk.*

2 *There are two chairs.*

3 _____

4 _____

5 _____

6 _____

7 _____

8 _____

Picture B

1 *There are two desks.*

2 *There's one chair.*

3 _____

4 _____

5 _____

6 _____

7 _____

8 _____

Progress check

1 Write the words with *a* or *an*.

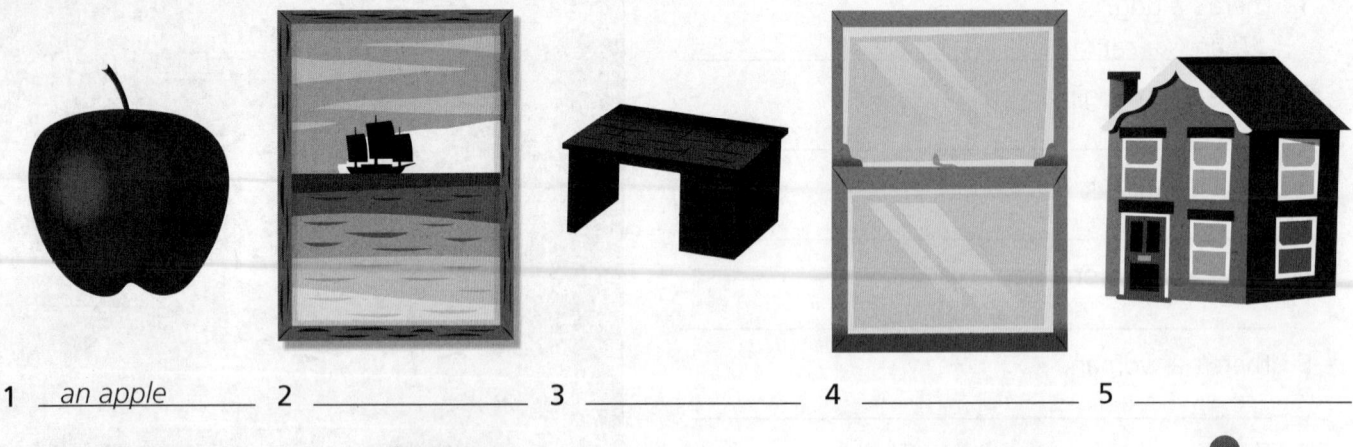

1 __*an apple*__ 2 _____ 3 _____ 4 _____ 5 _____

6 _____ 7 _____ 8 _____ 9 _____ 10 _____

2 Complete the dialogue. Put the words in the correct order.

	name's Hi, my Toby
	Hannah I'm Hi,
Toby	¹ *Hi, my name's Toby.*
Hannah	² _____.
	you that How spell do
	double N A H H A
Toby	³ _____?
Hannah	⁴ _____.
	your number What's telephone
	oh one seven four eight nine double
	two three four six It's
Toby	⁵ _____?
Hannah	⁶ _____
	_____
	_____46.
	you later See
	Goodbye, you see
Toby	⁷ _____!
Hannah	⁸ _____!

3 Put the words in the correct order.

1 exercise your book Open
   __*Open your exercise book.*__

2 up pencil Pick your
   _____

3 picture Look the at
   _____

4 to Go the board
   _____

5 Put your down pencil
   _____

6 the board on Write
   _____

7 morning' Say 'Good
   _____

8 book exercise your Close
   _____

4 Write the numbers.

1 19   _nineteen_
2 22   _____
3 40   _____
4 13   _____
5 50   _____
6 65   _____
7 70   _____
8 100   _____
9 11   _____
10 18   _____

5 🎧 1.6 Listen and write the phone numbers.

1 _01134960821_
2 _____
3 _____
4 _____
5 _____
6 _____

6 Correct the sentences.

1 There's one child.
   There are five children.

2 There are two cats.
   _____

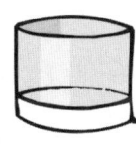

3 There's one person.
   _____

4 There's one glass.
   _____

5 There are three women.
   _____

6 There's one watch.
   _____

7 There's one man.
   _____

8 There are four toothbrushes.
   _____

I can ...

Write the answers and tick (✓) the correct box.

1 You   Hi! My _____. What's
             _____?
   Lily Hello. _____ Lily.
   You   How _____?
   Lily I _____, thanks.

I can introduce myself and ask who people are.

☐ Yes   ☐ I need more practice

2 three _____ five six
   twenty-five twenty-six _____ twenty-eight
   eighty-two _____ eighty-four _____

I can count 1 100.

☐ Yes   ☐ I need more practice

3 David _____ your phone _____?
   You   It's _____.

I can give and ask for telephone numbers.

☐ Yes   ☐ I need more practice

4 orange _____oranges_____
   child   _____
   man   _____
   glass   _____

I can use and make plurals.

☐ Yes   ☐ I need more practice

2 Friends and family

2A Where are you from?

Countries

1 ✴ **Match the countries to the pictures.**

1 Germany _b_   7 Russia _____
2 Brazil _____   8 France _____
3 Spain _____   9 Italy _____
4 the USA _____   10 Australia _____
5 Greece _____   11 Japan _____
6 Britain _____   12 China _____

a    b

c    d

e    f

g    h

i    j

k   l

2 ✴ **Find the countries from exercise 1.**

b	r	a	z	i	l	c	p	i	t	a	l	y	g
x	u	d	v	g	f	h	k	o	g	f	g	q	e
g	s	u	s	p	a	i	n	u	r	r	d	t	r
l	s	t	y	b	j	n	p	b	e	a	b	h	m
r	i	h	q	l	w	a	m	h	e	n	w	e	a
j	a	p	a	n	i	c	t	z	c	c	x	u	n
w	b	r	i	t	a	i	n	t	e	e	j	s	y
k	a	u	s	t	r	a	l	i	a	y	r	a	p

3 ✴✴ **Complete the bubbles.**

1 *I'm from France.*   ecanFr

2 _____   paSni

3 _____   siusRa

4 _____   tBniira

5 _____   hnaCi

6 _____   And you?

be

4 ★ **Complete the bubbles. Use the short forms.**

1 They are in Milan. _____They're_____ in Milan.

2 I am thirteen. _____ thirteen.

3 We are in Class 7. _____ in Class 7.

4 She is my Internet friend. _____ my Internet friend.

5 You are from Japan. _____ from Japan.

6 My name is Heidi. _____ Heidi.

5 ★★ **Complete the sentences. Use the short forms.**

Name	Country
May Ling	China
Francesca	Italy
Claudia and Pablo	Spain
Rafael	Brazil
Jacques and Marcel	France
Jens	Germany

1 May Ling __isn't__ from Italy.
  She's from _China_____ .

2 Francesca _____ from Britain.
  She _____ .

3 Claudia and Pablo _____ from Russia.
  They _____ .

4 Rafael _____ from China.
  He _____ .

5 Jacques and Marcel _____ from Spain.
  They _____ .

6 Jens _____ from Australia.
  He _____ .

Listening

6 ★★★ 🎧 1.7 Jessica is introducing herself. Listen. Are the statements true (✓) or false (✗)? Correct the false ones.

1 Jessica's middle name is Claire. ✗
  Jessica's middle name is Jade.

2 She's from Britain. ✓
  _____

3 Her house is in Liverpool. ☐
  _____

4 She's eleven. ☐
  _____

5 Her favourite group is JLS. ☐
  _____

6 Her Internet friends are from China. ☐
  _____

7 Their names are Mayumi and Hiroto. ☐
  _____

8 They are ten and thirteen years old. ☐
  _____

Writing

7 ★★★ **Read the text. Write a similar email about yourself.**

Hi! I'm Robert. My full name is Robert Thomas Wood. My nickname is 'Woody' – from my surname. I'm from the USA and my house is in Miami. I'm eleven years old. My favourite group is The Wanted. My friends at school are Tyler and James. Tyler is eleven and James is twelve.

_Hi! I'm ..._
_____
_____
_____
_____
_____

Family

1 ⬛ **Look at the family tree. Complete the bubbles.**

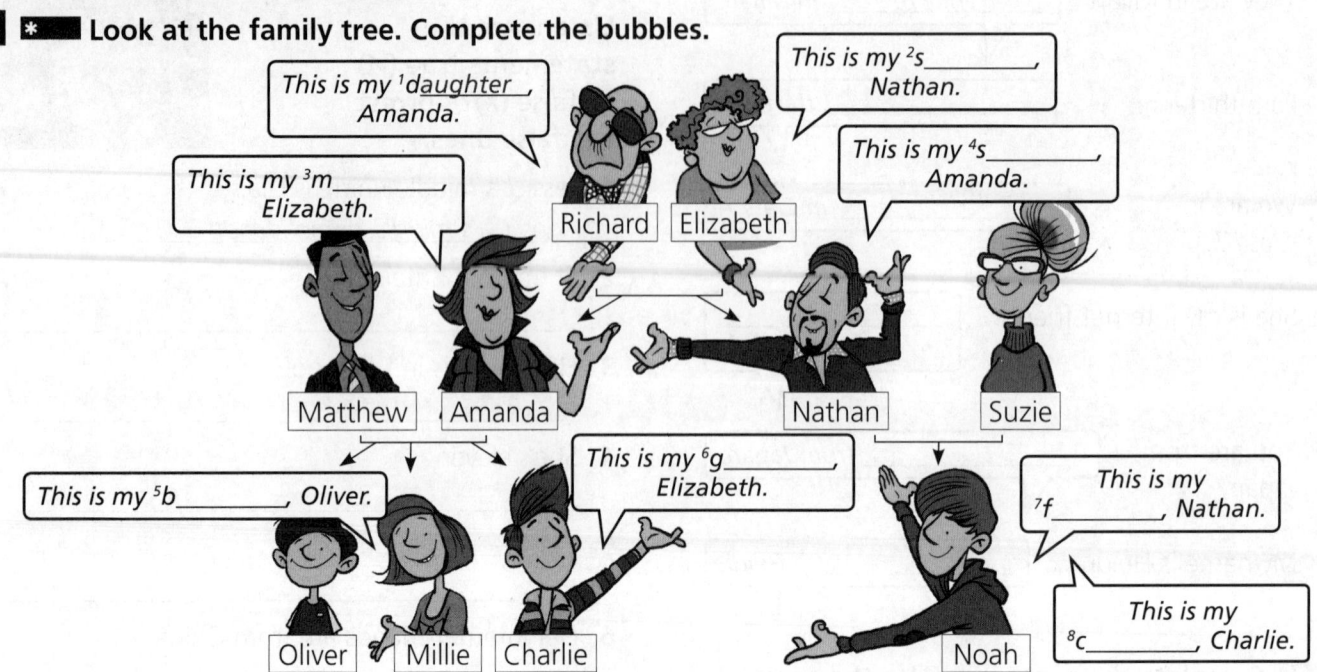

This is my ¹daughter, Amanda.

This is my ²s_____, Nathan.

This is my ³m_____, Elizabeth.

This is my ⁴s_____, Amanda.

Richard Elizabeth

Matthew Amanda Nathan Suzie

This is my ⁵b_____, Oliver.

This is my ⁶g_____, Elizabeth.

This is my ⁷f_____, Nathan.

Oliver Millie Charlie

Noah

This is my ⁸c_____, Charlie.

2 ✱✱ **Find ten family words.**

g	r	a	n	d	d	a	d	d
p	g	a	u	n	c	l	e	a
z	r	u	g	t	s	k	j	u
m	a	n	w	b	o	u	v	g
o	n	t	k	r	n	y	x	h
t	d	c	o	u	s	i	n	t
h	m	s	i	s	t	e	r	e
e	a	b	r	o	t	h	e	r
r	f	a	t	h	e	r	z	q

Possessive adjectives

3 ✱✱ **Write the answers.**

 Mark

 Jane

1 What's his name?
   His name's Mark.

2 What's her name?
   _____

 Leo

 Christina

3 What's his name?
   _____

4 What's her name?
   _____

 Freddie

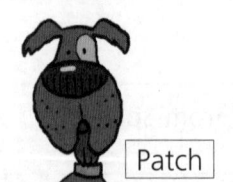 Patch

5 What's his name?
   _____

6 What's its name?
   _____

7 What's your name?
   _____

Possessive 's

4 ★ Put the ' in the correct place.

1 Oliver is _Millie's_ brother.
2 I'm Nathans sister.
3 This is your friends bag.
4 This is my teachers pen.
5 Marias bag is in the classroom.
6 This is Adams watch.
7 Our dogs name is Buddy.
8 We're in Granddad and Grandmas house.

Listening

5 a ★★ 🎧 1.8 Whose watch is this? Listen and match the names to the pictures.

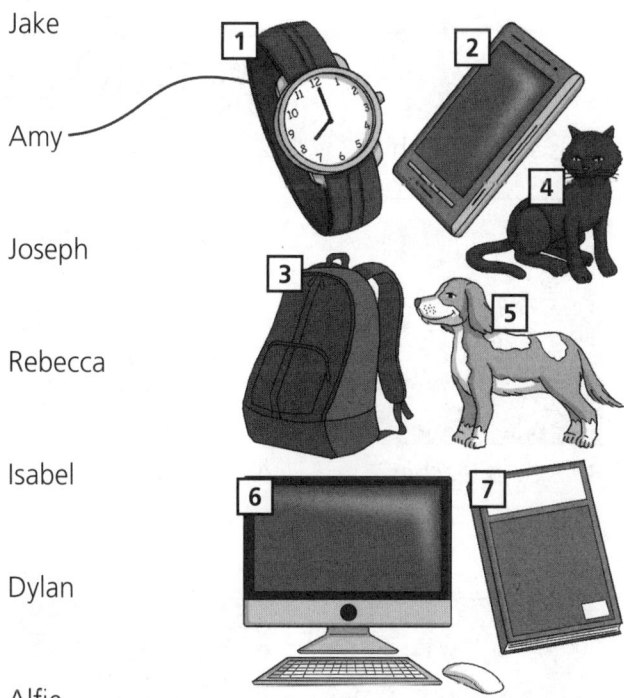

Jake

Amy

Joseph

Rebecca

Isabel

Dylan

Alfie

b Write sentences.

1 _This is Amy's watch._
2 _____
3 _____
4 _____
5 _____
6 _____
7 _____

6 ★★★ Complete the sentences with the possessive adjectives.

1 This is ___my___ Internet friend, and this is
   _____ d_____.

2 This is _____ c_____.

3 This is the Smiths' house. _____ c_____ is
   in the garden. _____ name is Fluffy.

4 This is _____ b_____. _____ name's
   Luke.

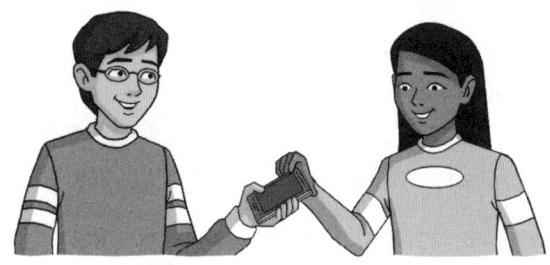

5 Here's _____ m_____ p_____.

be

1 ✷ ▬▬ **Complete the questions with *is* or *are*.**

1 • ___Is___ your name Ryan Smith?

2 • _____ you a film star?

3 • _____ you a singer, too?

4 • _____ he your son?

5 • _____ he fourteen years old?

6 • _____ you from the USA?

7 • _____ you from New York City?

8 • _____ your house in Manhattan?

9 • _____ your son's name Josh?

2 ✷✷ ▬ **Put the words in the correct order.**

1 your this dog Is

___Is this your dog?___

2 he Is friendly

_____?

3 Lara name your Is

_____?

4 sister Is your this

_____?

5 you Are London from

_____?

6 parents they Are your

_____?

7 Are twelve old years you

_____?

3 ✷ ▬▬ **Answer the questions about yourself. Use *Yes, I am* or *No, I'm not*.**

1 Are you eleven years old? ___No, I'm not.___

2 Are you from France? _____

3 Are you friendly? _____

4 Are you a boy? _____

5 Are you a girl? _____

6 Are you a student? _____

7 Are you ten years old? _____

4 ✷✷ ▬ **Write the answers.**

1 Is she from China? 2 Are they friendly?
  ___No, she isn't.___ _____

3 Is he a teacher? 4 Are you twelve?
_____ _____
  |

5 Is she on the computer? 6 Is it a dog?
_____ _____

7 Are you Harry? _____ |

5 ★★★ **Complete the questions and write the answers.**

1

> *Is* this an apple?

> No, it isn't. It's an orange.

2

> _____ this the Statue of Liberty?

> _____
> the Eiffel Tower.

3

> _____ this a pencil?

> _____

4

> _____ you from Greece?

> _____

5

> _____ your house in South Street?

> _____

Broad Street

Listening

6 a ★★★ **Write the questions.**

b 🎧 1.9 **Listen and answer the questions.**

Interviewer	1 *What's your name* ?
	(what / your / name)
Ben	My 2 *name's Ben* .
Interviewer	3_____? (how old / you)
Ben	I 4_____.
Interviewer	5_____? (this / your friend)
Ben	6_____, she _____. She _____.
Interviewer	7_____? (what / her / name)
Ben	Her 8_____.
Interviewer	9_____? (how old / she)
Ben	She 10_____.
Interviewer	11_____? (where / you / from)
Ben	We 12_____.
Interviewer	13_____? (you / from / Canberra)
Ben	14_____, we_____. We _____.

Days of the week

1 ✻ Find the days of the week.

j	t	z	u	n	b	k	o	t
k	u	f	r	i	d	a	y	h
m	e	s	t	l	b	k	w	u
o	s	u	n	d	a	y	h	r
n	d	x	j	f	y	d	e	s
d	a	w	k	i	a	j	z	d
a	y	q	h	s	t	g	p	a
y	s	a	t	u	r	d	a	y
w	e	d	n	e	s	d	a	y

2 ✻✻ Write what the DJ says. Write the numbers in words.

Name	Sam Walker
Where	London
Age	11
Song for	sister
Name	Kate
Where	home
Age	13

Name	Lisa Hall
Where	Manchester
Song for	granddad
Name	Simon
Age	58
Where	Spain

This song is from Sam, in ¹ __London__. Sam is ² _____ years old. The song is for his ³ _____, Kate. Kate is at ⁴ _____ today. It's her birthday. She's ⁵ _____! Happy birthday, Kate!

... And this song is from ⁶ _____, in ⁷ _____. It's for her ⁸ _____, Simon. He's ⁹ _____ today! Simon is in ¹⁰ _____. Hello, Simon!

Listening

3 ✻✻ 🎧 1.10 Listen and complete the dialogue with the words in the box.

Bye	~~boys~~	friend	Happy	here	home
old	song	photo	eleven	today	

Harvey Good morning, girls and ¹ __boys__! I'm Harvey, and this is *Favourite Songs*! Today, Jack is ² _____. Jack, who is in this ³ _____? Is he your brother?

Jack No, he isn't my brother. He's my ⁴ _____, Adam. It's his birthday ⁵ _____.

Harvey Is he at ⁶ _____?

Jack Yes, he is.

Harvey Oh! ⁷ _____ birthday, Adam! How ⁸ _____ is he, Jack?

Jack He's ⁹ _____.

Harvey OK. Has Adam got a favourite ¹⁰ _____?

Jack Yes, he has. It's Maroon 5's *Moves like Jagger*.

Harvey Here's the video for Adam.

Jack Thanks, Harvey. ¹¹ _____!

Wh- questions

4 ★ Circle the correct words.

1 **(What's)**/ **Who's** your name?

2 **How** / **Where** are you from?

3 **How** / **Who** old are you?

4 **Where** / **When** is your birthday?

5 **What** / **How** is your mobile phone number?

6 **Who** / **When** is your teacher?

7 **When** / **What** is your favourite book?

8 **Who** / **Where** is your house?

5 ★★ Put the words in the correct order to make questions. Write answers about yourself.

you   are   How
1   _How are you?_
    I'm fine thanks.

your   What   name   is
2   _____?
    _____

are   old   you   How
3   _____?
    _____

day   today   is   What   it
4   _____?
    _____

is   your   Who   teacher
5   _____?
    _____

your   When   birthday   is
6   _____?
    _____

friend's   your   What   name   is
7   _____?
    _____

you   today   are   Where
8   _____?
    _____

6 ★★★ Write questions for the answers.

1   _What's your name?_
    My name's Amelia.

2   _____?
    My brother's twelve.

3   _____?
    No, I'm not. I'm from Spain.

4   _____?
    It's on 5th February.

5   _____?
    My neighbour is Mrs Williams.

6   _____?
    My brother's name is Max.

7   _____?
    No, he isn't. He's a student.

8   _____?
    My friend is at home today.

Progress check

1 **Complete the sentences with the words in the box and the affirmative or negative of *be*. Use the short forms.**

| I (x2)   he (x2)   she (x2)   it   we   they (x2) |

1 My name's Olivia. ___I'm___ from the USA.

2 My brother is eighteen. _____ a student.

3 _____ my sister Grace's birthday today.

4 'How old is Grace?' '_____ fourteen.'

5 I'm at school today. _____ at home.

6 This is my teacher, Mr Brown. _____ from York.

7 My mum and dad are at the shops. _____ in the garden.

8 Angelina Jolie is a film star. _____ a singer.

9 These are my Internet friends. _____ from Brazil.

10 'Ruby and Lewis, where are you?' 'Here, Mum! _____ on the computer!'

2 **Complete the dialogue. Use a pronoun or possessive adjective.**

DJ	Hello. It's Friday. ¹___*My*___ name's Aisha Cox and this is *The Birthday Show*. Hi. What's ²_____ name?
Leon	Leon Harrison.
DJ	Hello, Leon. How old are ³_____?
Leon	⁴_____'m eleven.
DJ	And who is ⁵_____ song for?
Leon	It's for ⁶_____ sister, Mia.
DJ	When's ⁷_____ birthday?
Leon	It's on Monday.
DJ	And how old is ⁸_____?
Leon	⁹_____'s fourteen on Monday.
DJ	Where are ¹⁰_____?
Leon	¹¹_____'m at home with ¹²_____ dad. ¹³_____'s on ¹⁴_____ computer.
DJ	Hi, Leon's Dad! Is Mia there, too?
Leon	No, ¹⁵_____ isn't.
DJ	Well, happy birthday, Mia, from ¹⁶_____ brother Leon. Here's the song.

3 🎧 1.11 **Look at the picture. Listen and answer the questions. Use the short forms.**

1 • Is Paul in the photo?

  o *No, he isn't.* _____

2 • Is Paul's father a postman?

  o _____. He _____

3 • Is Paul's father's name John?

  o _____

4 • Is Paul's mother from the USA?

  o _____. She _____

5 • Is Paul's mother a singer?

  o _____

6 • Are Jim and Alice twelve?

  o _____. They _____

7 • Is Paul twelve?

  o _____

8 • In the photo, are they in their garden?

  o _____

4 Match the questions to the answers.

1 Where are you?   c
2 Are your friends at the shops?
3 Who's this?
4 Where are you from?
5 What's your name?
6 Is your dog friendly?
7 Where's 15 King Street?
8 When is your birthday?
9 Are you Lily, our new classmate?
10 How old is your grandmother?
11 Is your mother a famous film star?

a That's it – over there.
b No, she isn't.
c ~~In the garden.~~
d It's my friend, Keira.
e She's sixty.
f I'm Hugo.
g No, I'm not. I'm Charlotte.
h Yes, they are.
i On Saturday.
j Yes, he is.
k London, in England.

5 Complete the questions. Then write answers about yourself.

1 _What's_ _your_ name?
   My name's Helen.

2 _____ _____ _____ you?
_____

3 _____ _____ _____ from?
_____

4 _____ _____ eleven?
_____

5 _____ _____ birthday _____ Monday?
_____

6 _____ _____ phone _____?
_____

7 _____ _____ address?
_____

I can ...

Write the answers and tick (✓) the correct box.

1 You   Hello! I'm from _____. These are
       my Internet friends. _____ from
       _____. Where _____?
   Ivan   _____ Russia.

I can say and ask where people are from.
☐ Yes   ☐ I need more practice

2 Ted – bike   _This is Ted's bike._
   Mrs Wilson – book   _____
   my sister – mobile   _____
   Katy and Rod – house   _____

I can say who owns what.
☐ Yes   ☐ I need more practice

3 Write three sentences about your family.
_____
_____
_____
_____

I can talk about my family.
☐ Yes   ☐ I need more practice

4 Write questions for these answers.
_____? It's Friday today.
_____? It's on Saturday.
_____? No, it isn't. It's Monday.

I can ask questions and talk about the days of the week.
☐ Yes   ☐ I need more practice

3 My world

3A I've got a computer

Possessions

1 ✱✱ Label the pictures.

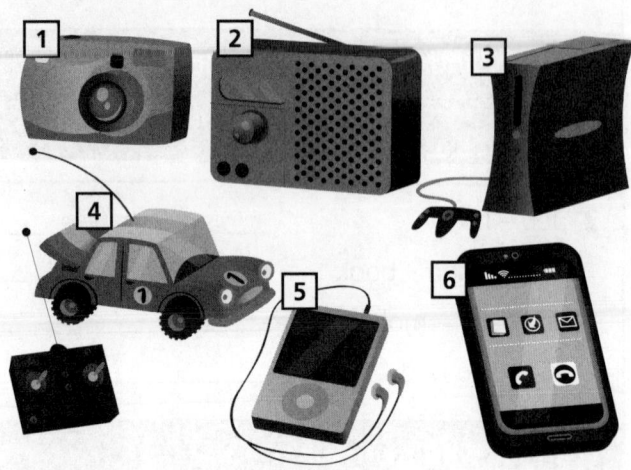

1 a <u>c a m e r a</u>

2 a _ _ _ _ _ _

3 a _ _ _ _ _ _ _ _ _ _ _ _ _ _ _ _

4 a _ _ _ _ _ _ _ _-
_ _ _ _ _ _ _ _ _ _ _ _ _ _

5 an _ _ _ _ _ _ _ _ _ _

6 a _ _ _ _ _ _ _ _ _ _ _ _

2 ✱✱ Find five more things.

d	k	h	o	y	w	q	t	o
s	p	m	s	k	i	d	e	c
k	c	a	m	e	r	a	l	o
a	w	e	y	v	p	x	e	m
t	n	q	v	n	t	m	v	p
e	w	b	i	k	e	h	i	u
b	r	t	m	e	w	y	s	t
o	x	v	i	u	s	k	i	e
a	s	e	p	d	i	h	o	r
r	u	n	b	w	o	b	n	d
d	v	d	p	l	a	y	e	r

Listening

3 ✱✱ 🎧 1.12 Listen and match the people to their presents. Complete the sentences.

Joshua

Sophie

Ed

Yasmin

Mum and Dad

Finley

1 Joshua has got _<u>a remote-controlled car</u>_.

2 Sophie has got _____.

3 Ed has got _____.

4 Yasmin has got _____.

5 Mum and Dad have got _____.

6 Finley has got _____.

have got / has got

4 ✱ Complete the sentences with 've or 's.

1 She*'s*_____ got a computer.

2 I_____ got three brothers.

3 Asif_____ got a DVD player.

4 We_____ got mobile phones.

5 My sister_____ got a camera.

6 They_____ got two televisions.

7 David_____ got a good skateboard.

8 You_____ got a nice bike.

5 ✱ Make the sentences negative.

1 Sarah's got a bike.

Sarah hasn't got a bike.

2 We've got a skateboard.

_____

3 You've got a radio at home.

_____

4 Theo's got ten DVDs.

_____

5 They've got a computer.

_____

6 The teacher's got my mobile phone.

_____

7 We've got a DVD player in our classroom.

_____

8 I've got a camera in my bag.

_____

is or has?

6 ✱✱ Write the full sentences.

1 Mark's got a DVD player.

Mark has got a DVD player.

2 She's from London.

_____

3 Georgia's got a television in her bedroom.

_____

4 He's got forty DVDs.

_____

5 My sister's eleven.

_____

6 She's in the living room.

_____

7 Megan's got a cat.

_____

8 Its name's Tillie.

_____

have got / has got

7 ✱✱✱ Look at the pictures. Correct the sentences.

1 Toby / bike

Toby hasn't got a bike.
He's got a skateboard.

2 Esme / radio

_____

_____

3 Freddie / MP3 player

_____

_____

4 Karl and Adam / computer

_____

_____

5 Nicole / DVD player

_____

_____

6 Nathan / television

_____

_____

7 They / camera

_____

3B Mut's present

Colours

1 ★ **Find seven more colours.**

whitehkuazgreenilhvborangetuocbluekredyopmewyellowsdbrownokpblackaftn

Listening

2 ★★ 🎧 1.13 **Listen and colour the pictures.**

Adjectives

3 ★ **Match the words in A to the opposites in B.**

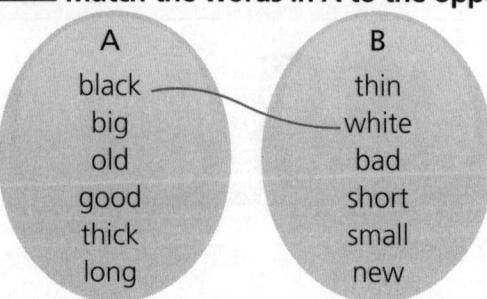

A	B
black	thin
big	white
old	bad
good	short
thick	small
long	new

4 ★★ **Describe these things. Use the words in the box.**

big good thick short small
old thin bad new long

1 *This is a big television.* _____

2 _____ _____

3 _____ _____

4 _____ _____

5 _____ _____

5 ** Put the words in the correct order.

1 blue pen is This my
   This is my blue pen.

2 a long They've car got
   _____

3 present a big is This
   _____

4 got a teacher I've good
   _____

5 at jumper Look my thick
   _____

6 bike new a This is
   _____

7 cats She's white got three
   _____

8 my Where's T-shirt green?
   _____

6 *** Look at the pictures. Correct the sentences.

1 They've got an old car.
   They haven't got an old car.
   They've got a new car.

2 She's got a thick jumper.
   _____
   _____

3 He's got a small bag.
   _____
   _____

4 They've got a new camera.
   _____
   _____

5 He's a bad boy.
   _____
   _____

6 She's got a black MP3 player.
   _____
   _____

Writing

7 *** Write about your things.
   I've got a bike. It's red and blue. It's new.
   I haven't got an MP3 player.
   _____
   _____
   _____
   _____
   _____
   _____
   _____
   _____
   _____
   _____
   _____

Have you got a pet?

Pets

1 ✱ ▬▬ **Complete the crossword with the words in the box.**

rabbit ~~hamster~~ snake rat spider horse mouse fish parrot budgie cat dog

Across

2

4

6

7

8

Down

1

3

5

7

9

Crossword grid:
```
1 h       2       3
4 a
  m
  s           5
6 t       7
  e
8 r    9
       10
11
```

2 ✱✱ ▬▬ **Write sentences.**

1 Emma *'s got two hamsters.*
2 Alisha _____
3 Jamie _____
4 Martha _____
5 Will _____
6 Jessica _____
7 Matthew _____

EMMA ALISHA JAMIE MARTHA WILL JESSICA MATTHEW

have got: questions and short answers

3 ✱▬▬ **Match the questions to the answers.**

1 [b] Have your grandparents got a car?

2 ☐ Have you got a computer?

3 ☐ Has your aunt got a black cat?

4 ☐ Have we got a nice classroom?

5 ☐ Has your dog got a blanket?

6 ☐ Has your brother got a mobile phone?

7 ☐ Have your cousins got a parrot?

a No, I haven't.

b ~~Yes, they have.~~

c Yes, we have.

d Yes, it has.

e No, they haven't.

f No, she hasn't.

g Yes, he has.

4 ✱✱▬ **Write questions. Give short answers about yourself.**

1 you / an Internet friend

Have you got an Internet friend?

Yes, I have. / No, I haven't.

2 you / a dog

_____?

_____

3 you / a skateboard

_____?

_____

4 you / brothers and sisters

_____?

_____

5 you / an MP3 player

_____?

_____

6 you / a rabbit

_____?

_____

Listening

5 a ✱✱✱ 🎧 1.14 **Amy is talking about her friends, the Jackson family. Listen and complete the table.**

Name	Pet?	Type of pet
Amy	Yes / (No)	
Lily	(Yes) / No	*A dog*
Peter	Yes / No	
Tom	Yes / No	
Andrew	Yes / No	
Mr and Mrs Jackson	Yes / No	

b Write sentences.

1 Amy _hasn't got a pet._

2 Lily *'s got a pet. She's got a dog.*

3 Peter _____

4 Tom _____

5 Andrew _____

6 Mr and Mrs Jackson _____

3D My school

School subjects

1 ✱⬛⬛ Label the subjects with the words from the box.

Biology   Chemistry   ~~Citizenship~~   Design and Technology   English   Geography   ICT   Maths   Music   RE

1 _Citizenship_   2 _____   3 _____   4 _____   5 _____

6 _____   7 _____   8 _____   9 _____   10 _____

Listening

2 ✱✱⬛ 🎧 (1.15) Ellie and Adam are talking about their new timetable. Listen and complete.

	Monday	Tuesday	Wednesday	Thursday	Friday
9.00 – 10.00	[1] _Art and Design_	Maths	[4] _____	Music	Physics
10.05 – 11.05	English	Maths	[5] _____	Biology	English
11.20 – 12.20	English	[3] _____	Citizenship	[6] _____	ICT
12.20 – 1.20	LUNCH				
1.20 – 2.20	Geography	Physics	English	Geography	Maths
2.25 – 3.25	[2] _____	Biology	Chemistry	Technology	[7] _____

3 ✱✱✱ Look at the pictures and complete the text.

Hello! My name's Cara. I'm in class 8L at Priory

[1] _School_  . There are 900 [2]_____

 at my school! We wear a [3]_____

 – it's blue and grey.

Priory is a nice school. The [4]_____

are good, and they are very [5]_____ 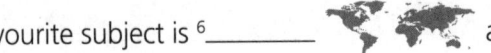 .

My favourite subject is [6]_____ 🗺️ and

I'm good at [7] _____ 🏴󠁧󠁢󠁥󠁮󠁧󠁿 , too.

I'm not very good at [8]_____ 🧪 or

Physics but [9]_____ 🌷 with Mrs Jenkins

on Thursdays is great.

My favourite day at school is Friday. We've got

[10]  in the afternoon with Mrs

Andrews. She's very nice.

4 ✱✱ Write the names of the lessons. Then write the day you've got the subjects.

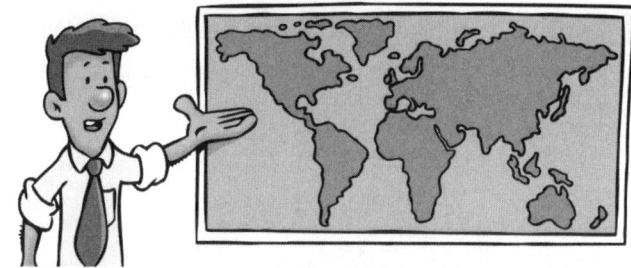

> **Be**
>
> I am — We are
> You are — You are
> He/She/It is — They are

1   _English. We've got English on Monday._

6   _____

2   _____

7   _____

3   _____

8   _____

4   _____

5   _____

Writing

5 ✱✱✱ Write about your school and timetable. Use the phrases in the box and your own ideas, too.

> My name's …   I'm in class …   My school subjects are …   My favourite subject is …   We've got this subject on …   I'm good at …   I'm bad at …
> My favourite day at school is …

_____

_____

_____

_____

_____

_____

_____

Progress check

1 Look at the two pictures of Ben's room. Write the things that are different in picture B.

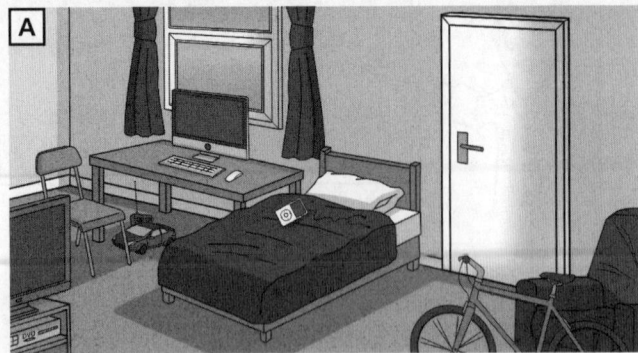

In picture B …

1 *Ben hasn't got a television. He's got a radio.*

2 _____

3 _____

4 _____

5 _____

6 _____

2 Describe these things. Use the words in the box.

friendly   long   new   old
good   big   ~~thick~~   thin

1   *a thick book*   2 _____

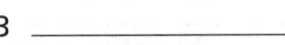

3 _____   4 _____

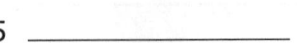

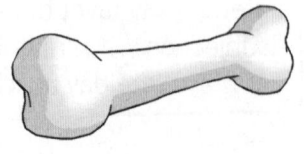

5 _____   6 _____

7 _____   8 _____

3 Read the text and answer the questions.

The Jordan family have got ten pets. Emma's got a big white rabbit – it's very friendly but it's always asleep. She's got a small blue and yellow budgie, too. Her sister Kate's got a big horse. Her brother Alfie's got a black rabbit and a white rat. Mum and Dad have got two small dogs. Their names are Buster and Sammy. They've got a black and white cat, too. Grandma and Granddad have got two green parrots – Bill and Ben.

1 Have the Jordan family got nine pets?
  No, they haven't.

2 What pets has Emma got?
_____

3 Has Kate got a small pet?
_____

4 Has Alfie got two pets?
_____

5 What pets have Mum and Dad got?
_____

6 Have Grandma and Granddad got two green birds?
_____

4 **Write the subjects.**

1 tra dan isnged   *Art and Design*
2 perhgyoga   _____
3 suicm   _____
4 lighsne   _____
5 amsht   _____
6 iyohrts   _____
7 hcmyersit   _____
8 cpysish   _____

5 (🎧 1.16) **Charlotte is talking about her school. Listen and choose the correct answers.**

1 The school is in __*a*__.
   a London   b Liverpool
   c Los Angeles   d Lisbon

2 At the school, there are _____ students.
   a 100   b 200
   c 300   d 400

3 Charlotte has got _____ every day.
   a Maths   b French
   c Music   d Geography

4 She has got English on _____ and Wednesday.
   a Monday   b Tuesday
   c Thursday   d Friday

5 Her favourite subject is _____.
   a ICT   b Art and Design
   c PE   d Music

6 On Friday afternoon she's got _____ and ICT.
   a Maths   b French
   c Science   d Art and Design

I can ...

Write the answers and tick (✓) the correct box.

1 I: radio (✓) mobile (✗). I _____ got a
   radio, but I _____ a mobile.
   My father: MP3 player (✗) computer (✓).
   My father _____
   _____.

I can talk about the things I've got and the things other people have got.

☐ Yes   ☐ I need more practice

2 I've got a 🐶 _____. My friend's got
   two 🐰 _____ and a 🐴 _____.

I can talk about pets.

☐ Yes   ☐ I need more practice

3 My English book is orange and _____.
   My exercise book is _____.

I can say the names of colours and give simple descriptions.

☐ Yes   ☐ I need more practice

4 I like **34+12 = 46** _____, but my
   favourite subject is ✏ _____.

I can talk about school subjects.

☐ Yes   ☐ I need more practice

Listening

1 * 🎧 1.17 **Listen. Draw the hands on the clocks and watches.**

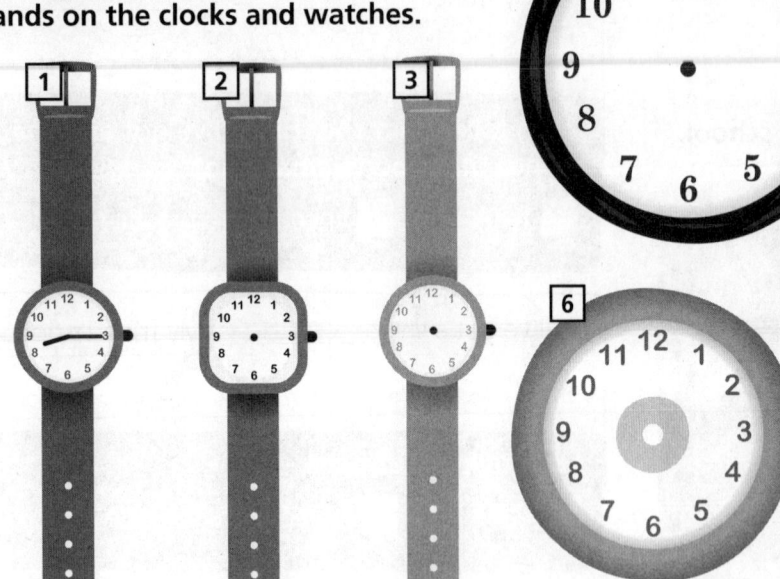

2 ** **Write the times.**

1 _It's twelve o'clock._
2 _____
3 _____
4 _____
5 _____
6 _____
7 _____
8 _____
9 _____
10 _____
11 _____
12 _____

Prepositions of time

3 ★★ **Write on or at.**

1 It's my birthday __on__ Sunday.
2 The party is _____ quarter to seven.
3 Your music lesson is _____ Thursday.
4 Is the match _____ three o'clock?
5 Our Maths exam is _____ Friday morning.
6 Ellen's hockey game is _____ half past two.
7 The school concert is _____ Saturday evening.
8 Have we got PE _____ Tuesday afternoon?
9 Is Harry's football match _____ 6.30?
10 The volleyball match is _____ Sunday.

4 **Read the diary and answer the questions. Write the times in words. Use on or at.**

MONDAY	football match at school 4.15
TUESDAY	cousin Philip's birthday party 6.30
WEDNESDAY	music concert school 7.00
THURSDAY	piano lesson 5.00
FRIDAY	piano exam 3.15

1 What time is Ollie's football match on Monday?
   The football match _is at quarter past four._
2 What day is his cousin's birthday party?
   His cousin's birthday party
   _____.
3 What time is the party?
   The party _____.
4 What day is the music concert at school?
   The music concert _____.
5 What time is the concert?
   The concert _____.
6 What day is the piano lesson?
   The piano lesson _____.
7 What time is his piano exam on Friday?
   His piano exam _____.

5 ★★★ **Put the words in the correct order to make questions. Then look at the picture and complete the dialogues.**

Monday		school concert
Tuesday		football match
Wednesday		hockey match
Thursday		volleyball match
Friday		class party
Saturday		Mark's violin exam
Sunday		tennis game

1 is match When hockey your
Susie _When is your hockey match?_
Nathan _It's at quarter to five on Wednesday._

2 concert on Is the school Monday
Nathan _____?
Susie _____

3 you your volleyball match Friday got Have on
Susie _____?
Nathan _____

4 Mark's exam When's violin
Susie _____?
Nathan _____

5 Friday a game on tennis we got Have
Nathan _____?
Susie _____

6 is party When the class
Nathan _____?
Susie _____

Vocabulary

1 ✱ **Find ten more words.**

1 _brush_   7 _____
2 _bus_   8 _____
3 _____   9 _____
4 _____   10 _____
5 _____   11 _____
6 _____   12 _____

Present simple: affirmative

2 ✱✱ **Look at the pictures of Oscar's day. Complete the sentences.**

1 _I get up at quarter to eight._

2 I _____ breakfast at
_____.

3 I _____ the bus to
_____ at _____.

4 Lessons _____ at _____
_____.

5 I _____ school at _____
_____.

6 I _____ my homework from
_____ to _____.

7 I _____ dinner at
_____.

8 I _____ TV from _____
to _____.

9 I _____ to bed at
_____.

Present simple: negative

3 ★★ **Write sentences with the negative form.**

1 I have a shower at seven o'clock.
   I don't have a shower at seven o'clock.

2 I have breakfast with my family.
   _____
   _____

3 My friends and I take the bus to school.
   _____
   _____

4 Lessons start at half past nine.
   _____
   _____

5 We finish school at quarter past three.
   _____
   _____

6 I watch TV with my sister.
   _____
   _____

7 We do our homework before dinner.
   _____
   _____

8 I go to bed at quarter past eight.
   _____
   _____

Listening

4 ★★ 🎧 1.18 **Listen to Rosie and Kate's day. Choose the correct answers.**

1 Rosie and Kate get up at __b__.
   a 7.00   b 7.10   c 7.30
2 They have breakfast at _____.
   a 7.30   b 7.40   c 7.45

3 They take the bus with _____.
   a their friends   b their parents
   c their brother
4 At school, lessons start at _____.
   a 9.00   b 9.15   c 9.20
5 At one o'clock they _____.
   a go home   b have a school dinner
   c have a packed lunch
6 At home, they _____ before dinner.
   a do homework   b watch football
   c read a book
7 After dinner, they watch TV with _____.
   a their parents   b their brothers
   c their friends
8 They go to bed at _____.
   a 8.45   b 9.30   c 9.45

Writing

5 ★★★ **Write about a typical day in your life. Use the words in the box and your own ideas, too.**

> shower   breakfast   teeth
> school   lessons   lunch
> home   dinner   homework
> TV   book   bed

I get up at ...
_____
_____
_____
_____
_____
_____
_____
_____
_____
_____
_____
_____
_____

4C Free time

Free time activities

1 ★ ■ ■ **Match the words in the box to the pictures.**

volleyball ice hockey violin tennis ~~football~~
computer games swimming badges piano
guitar skiing dance class

1 _____football_____

2 _____

3 the _____

4 _____

5 _____

6 the _____

7 _____

8 _____

9 _____

10 the _____

11 _____

12 _____

2 ★★ ■ **Put the words from exercise 1 in the correct column.**

play	go	collect
football	to	

3 ★★ ■ **What do they do in their free time? Write sentences with *play*, *go* or *collect*.**

1 Karen and Sarah
go to dance class.

2 Joe and Kate
_____.

3 Freddie and Ed
_____.

4 Megan and Anna
_____.

5 Tom and Will
_____.

6 David and Mike
_____.

Present simple: endings

4 ★ ■ ■ **Circle the correct words.**

1 Mr Miller **(likes)** / **like** sport.

2 Victoria **collects** / **collect** badges.

3 They **plays** / **play** tennis on Saturdays.

4 He **watches** / **watch** DVDs after school.

5 Lucas and Matt **goes** / **go** skiing.

6 I **gets up** / **get up** at half past seven.

7 My brother **goes** / **go** swimming with his friends.

8 Erin **plays** / **play** the piano at home.

Listening

5 a ✱✱ 🎧 1.19 **What does Billy do? Listen and write (✓) or (✗).**

	Billy
play football	✓
play tennis	
go swimming	
have music lessons	
play the piano	
watch football on TV	
collect badges	
play computer games	

b Write affirmative or negative sentences.

1 _Billy plays football._
2 _____
3 _____
4 _____
5 _____
6 _____
7 _____
8 _____

6 ✱✱✱ **Correct the sentences.**

We work in a school.

1 They _don't work in a school. They work in a shop._
_____

I play the piano after school.

2 He _____
_____

We have coffee for breakfast.

3 They _____
_____

The party starts at half past six.

Come to my party on Saturday from six o'clock to ten o'clock

4 The party _____

I get up at ten to nine.

5 She _____
_____

I do my homework in my bedroom.

6 He _____
_____

Music and sports

1 ✱ **Complete the sentences about yourself.**

1 My father plays _tennis and football._
2 I play _____.
3 I don't play _____.

4 My friend plays _____.
5 My friend doesn't play _____.
6 My favourite sport is _____.

2 ✱✱ **Complete the crossword.**

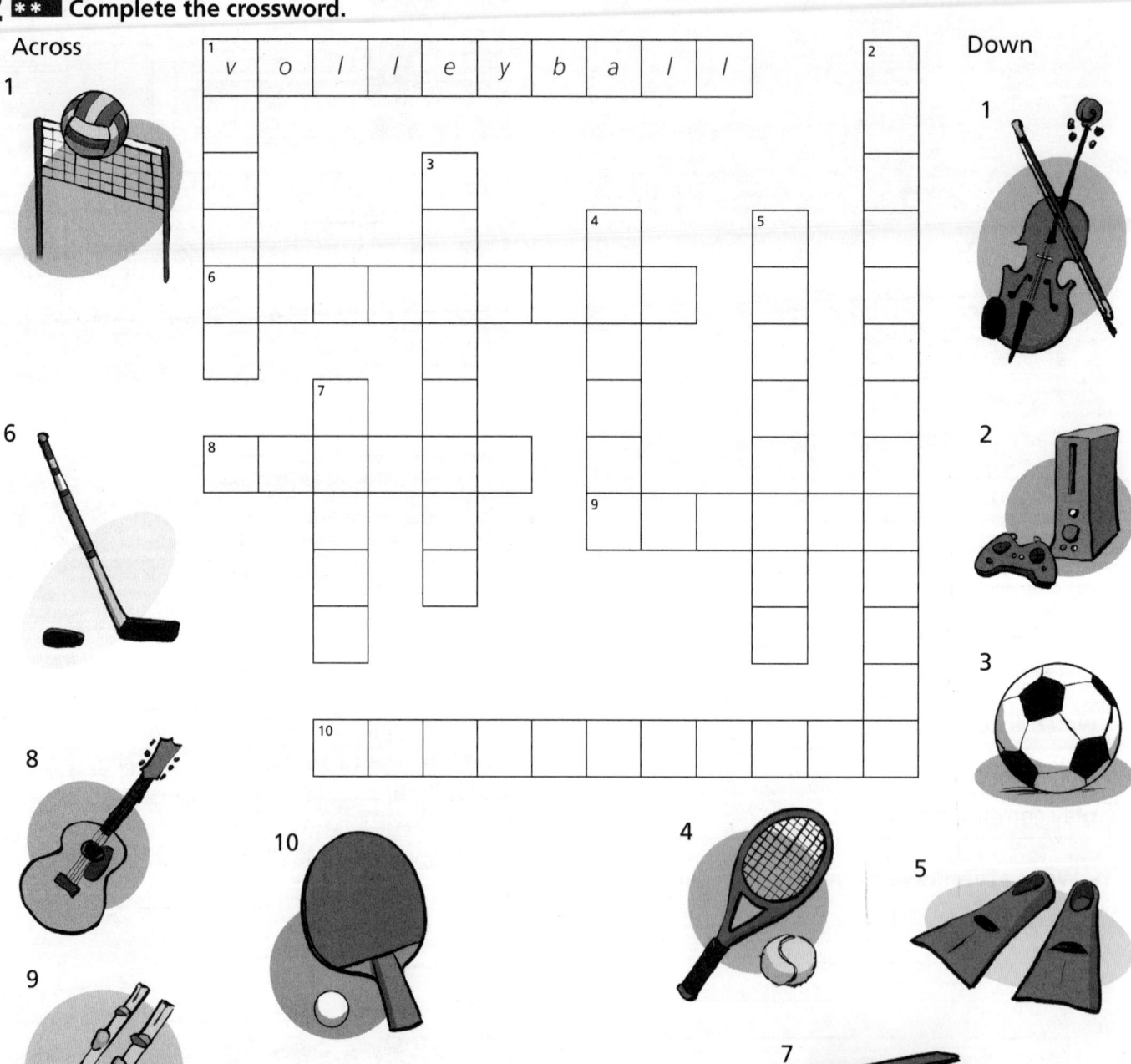

Across

1

6

8

9

Down

1

2

3

4

5

7

10

Present simple: questions and short answers

3 ✱ Complete the questions with *Do* or *Does*.

1 _Does_ Jake like volleyball?
2 _____ your friends go to football matches?
3 _____ our lessons start at nine o'clock?
4 _____ Amelia collect badges?
5 _____ they listen to the radio in the kitchen?
6 _____ your brother play table tennis?
7 _____ the dog go to the park with you?
8 _____ you go to dance class?
9 _____ your granddad watch sport on TV?
10 _____ we collect old comics?

Present simple: *Wh-* questions

4 ✱✱ Put the words in the correct order to make questions.

1 Bradley does When up get
   When does Bradley get up?
   He gets up at seven o'clock.
2 and Nina Lily When school start do
   _____?
   They start school at nine o'clock.
3 play volleyball Rashid does Where
   _____?
   He plays volleyball at school.
4 does the radio to When mum your listen
   _____?
   She listens to the radio in the morning.
5 lunch friends Where your do have
   _____?
   They have lunch at school.
6 TV you watch do When
   _____?
   I watch TV after dinner.
7 your live cousin does Where
   _____?
   He lives in Manchester.
8 piano does Ava her have lesson When
   _____?
   She has her piano lesson on Thursdays.

Listening

5 ✱✱✱ 🎧 1.20 Ivan is talking about his favourite things. Listen. Are the statements true (✓) or false (✗)?

1 Ivan collects badges. ✗
2 He plays football and table tennis. ☐
3 He plays computer games after school. ☐
4 He likes dance. ☐
5 He listens to the radio on Sundays. ☐
6 He plays the violin and the piano. ☐
7 He likes Maths. ☐
8 His favourite subjects are History and Geography. ☐

Writing

6 ✱✱✱ Answer the questions about yourself.

1 What do you do after school?
   I play tennis or watch TV with my friends.
2 When do you do your homework?
   _____
   _____
3 What does your mum do in her free time?
   _____
   _____
4 What sports do you play?
   _____
   _____
5 What do you do on Sundays?
   _____
   _____
6 What does your dad do on Saturday mornings?
   _____
   _____

Progress check

1 Write the questions and the answers. Write the times in words.

1 school concert: 8.00

• *When is the school concert?*

○ It's *at eight o'clock.*

2 the Maths exam: 4.15

• _____?

○ It's _____.

3 our volleyball match: 10.30

• _____?

○ It's _____.

4 the hockey game: 11.10

• _____?

○ It's _____.

5 Maria's swimming lesson: 11.50–12.40

• _____?

○ It's from _____ to _____.

6 Harvey's birthday party: 17.15

• _____?

○ It's _____.

2 Write about Dan's week.

Monday

get up

walk to school

play football with Mark

Tuesday

have a violin lesson

Wednesday

have dinner at his friend's house

Thursday

play tennis

Friday

go swimming with Mark

Saturday

go to the sports centre

1 *On Monday, he gets up at half past seven.*

2 _____

_____

3 On Monday, Dan and Mark _____

_____

4 _____

_____

5 _____

_____

6 _____

_____

7 _____

_____

8 _____

_____

3 a 🎧 1.21 **What do they do in their free time? Listen and write (✓) or (✗).**

1 Joel ☒ ☐

2 Clara ☐ ☐

3 Samira ☐ ☐

4 Max and Adam ☐ ☐

5 Isaac ☐ ☐

b Write affirmative or negative sentences.

1 Joel / computer games
   Joel doesn't play computer games.

2 Clara / the guitar
   _____

3 Samira / skiing
   _____

4 Max and Adam / football
   _____

5 Isaac / tennis
   _____

4 Put the words in the correct order to make questions. Then answer the questions about yourself.

1 you Do the play guitar ?
   Do you play the guitar?   *No , I don't.*

2 dinner you When have do
   _____?
   _____

3 your mother play piano Does the
   _____?
   _____

4 your What father play sports does
   _____?
   _____

I can ...

Write the answers and tick (✓) the correct box.

1 My _____ 🎻 lesson is at
   _____. 🕐

   I _____ 🎾 from
   _____ 🕐 to
   _____. 🕐

I can tell the time and say when things are.
☐ Yes   ☐ I need more practice

2 a shower: 🕐   *I have a shower*
                at 8 o'clock.

   breakfast: 🕐 _____
                  _____

   to school: 🕐 _____
                  _____

   homework: 🕐 _____
                 _____

I can talk about daily routines.
☐ Yes   ☐ I need more practice

3 My friend _____. (play)

   My friend _____. (not play)

I can talk about my friends and family.
☐ Yes   ☐ I need more practice

4 Ben What *sports do you play* ?
   You _____.
   Ben When _____?
   You _____.

I can ask and talk about free time activities.
☐ Yes   ☐ I need more practice

5 Places

5A My room

Things in a room

1 ✱ Label the things in Hannah's bedroom with the words in the box.

bed   bedside table   carpet   chair
chest of drawers   desk   ~~wardrobe~~   rug

1 _a wardrobe_   2 _____
3 _____   4 _____
5 _____   6 _____
7 _____   8 _____

2 ✱✱ Find seven things you can have in your room.

n	b	c	a	r	p	e	t	t	m
p	e	s	q	h	e	t	f	y	i
o	d	g	l	a	m	p	d	c	r
s	w	a	r	d	r	o	b	e	r
t	i	b	l	r	g	a	i	b	o
e	k	y	c	u	u	f	m	g	r
r	p	f	e	g	s	u	z	l	j
b	o	o	k	s	h	e	l	f	u

3 ✱✱ Look at the picture in exercise 1 and complete the bubbles.

1 Hannah does her homework at her ___desk___.

2 Hannah's clock is on her _____.

3 There are books on Hannah's _____.

4 Hannah sleeps in her _____.

5 There's a magazine behind Hannah's _____.

6 Hannah listens to her MP3 player on the _____.

7 There's a _____ next to Hannah's desk.

8 Hannah's old cat sits under her _____.

Listening

4 ✱✱ 🎧 1.22 Listen and draw a teddy bear in the correct place.

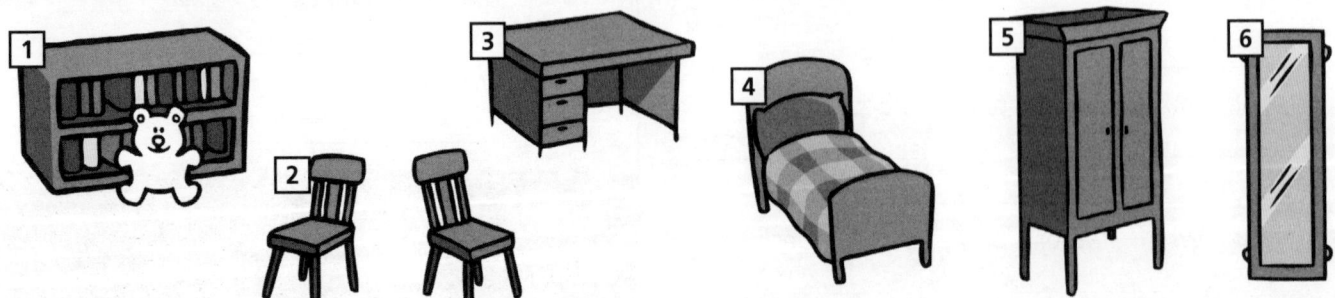

Prepositions of place

5 ★★ **Look at the picture. Are the statements true (✓) or false (✗)? Correct the false ones.**

1 The wardrobe is next to the bed. ✓

_____

2 The magazines are on the chest of drawers. ✗
  The magazines are on the table.

3 The bed is in front of the wardrobe. ☐

_____

4 The football is behind the wardrobe. ☐

_____

5 The box is on the bed. ☐

_____

6 The table is in front of the wardrobe. ☐

_____

7 The rug is under the chest of drawers. ☐

_____

8 The violin is between the bed and the ☐
  chest of drawers.

_____

6 ★★ **Look at the picture again. Complete the sentences. Use on, in, under, behind, next to or between.**

1 The lamp is _____on_____ the chest of drawers.
2 The bag is _____ the wardrobe.
3 The DVDs are _____ the table.
4 The teddy bear is _____ the wardrobe.
5 The mirror is _____ the wardrobe.
6 The mobile is _____ the chest of drawers.
7 The bed is _____ the chest of drawers
  and the wardrobe.

7 ★★★ **Where are their houses? Read and find the children's houses.**

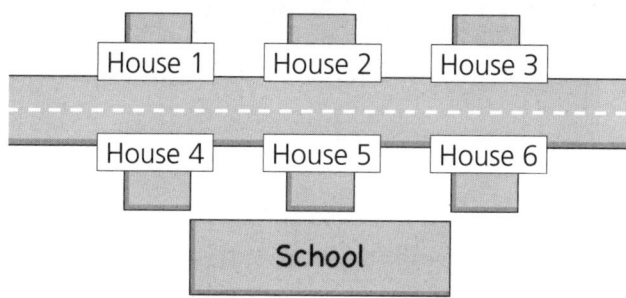

Lucy's house is next to Owen's house. Owen's house is between Lucy's house and Mia's house. Robert's house is next to Leo's house. Leo's house is opposite Owen's house. Jake's house is opposite Lucy's house and next to Leo's house. The school is in front of Jake, Leo and Robert's houses.

1 __Lucy__   2 _____   3 _____
4 _____   5 _____   6 _____

8 ★★★ **Close your eyes. Think about your classroom at school. Answer the questions.**

1 What have you got in your school bag?
  I've got three books and my lunch.

2 Where is your desk?

_____

3 Who is sitting in front of you?

_____

4 Who is sitting behind you?

_____

5 What have you got on your desk?

_____

6 Where is the teacher?

_____

7 What is next to the window?

_____

Rooms in a house

1 a ✳▇▇ Label the parts of the house with the words in the box.

9 _____

10 _____

11

16

12

15

13

14

1 _bedroom_

2 _____

3 _____

17

19   20

18

4 _____

5 _____

6 _____

7 _____

8 _____

21   22

---

armchair bath bathroom ~~bedroom~~ cooker
cupboard curtains   dining room downstairs
fridge garden hall kitchen stairs light
living room shower sink sofa toilet
upstairs washbasin

b Complete the list of furniture and things
with the words in the box.

11 _____   17 _____

12 _____   18 _____

13 _____   19 _____

14 _____   20 _____

15 _____   21 _____

16 _____   22 _____

2 ✳✳▇▇ **Where do you do these things? Write
sentences.**

1 have breakfast
   I have breakfast in the kitchen.

2 watch DVDs
   _____

3 have dinner
   _____

4 read books
   _____

5 brush your teeth
   _____

6 do your homework
   _____

7 have a shower
   _____

8 listen to music
   _____

There is / are

3 ☀ ▬▬ **Look at the picture of the house in exercise 1. Complete the sentences with *There's* or *There are*.**

1 _There's_ a wardrobe in the bedroom.

2 _____ a shower in the bathroom.

3 _____ two bedrooms.

4 _____ cupboards in the kitchen.

5 _____ a man in the kitchen.

6 _____ a big table in the dining room.

7 _____ two armchairs in the living room.

8 _____ a chest of drawers in the bedroom.

4 ▬▬▬ **Complete the text with *'s*, *isn't*, *are* or *aren't*.**

I live here! There ¹'s_____ only one room. It's a kitchen, dining room, living room and bedroom! There ²_____ three beds. One bed ³_____ in a drawer! There ⁴_____ a wardrobe, too. It's next to the beds. There ⁵_____ a desk, but there ⁶_____ a table. I do my homework at this table and we eat here, too. The room is small so there ⁷_____ big posters on the walls. There ⁸_____ a bathroom in my home, too. Where do I live?

Listening

5 ▬▬▬ 🎧 1.23 **David is talking about his house. Listen and answer the questions.**

1 Is the house big or small?
   It's small.

2 Have they got a dining room?
   _____

3 Where is David's bedroom?
   _____

4 Has David got a computer in his bedroom?
   _____

5 Where is the television?
   _____

6 What is next to David's bedroom?
   _____

7 What is in the bathroom?
   _____

8 Have they got a garden?
   _____

5C Our town

Places in a town

1 ✱ Label the places.

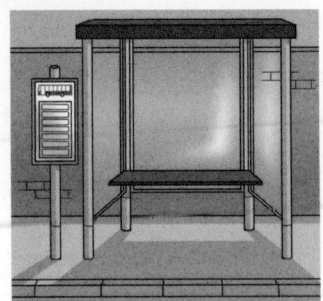   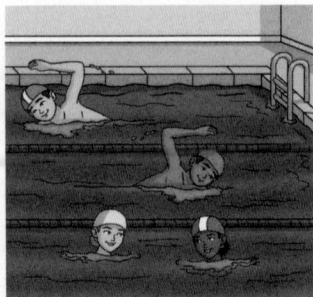

1 a b _us_ s _top_ 2 a t_____ 3 a s_____ 4 a s_____
c_____ p_____

5 a p_____ 6 a s_____ 7 a s_____ 8 a h_____
o_____ c_____

There is / are: questions

2 ✱✱ Look at the picture. Make dialogues about the town.

1 cinema
- • _Is there a cinema?_
- ○ _Yes, there is._

2 two banks
- • _Are there two banks?_
- ○ _No, there aren't._

3 a museum
- • _____ ?
- ○ _____

4 a swimming pool
- • _____ ?
- ○ _____

5 a church
- • _____ ?
- ○ _____

6 two cafés
- • _____ ?
- ○ _____

7 two supermarkets
- • _____ ?
- ○ _____

Prepositions of place

3 ****** **Look at the picture in exercise 2. Complete the sentences with _in front of_, _behind_, _between_, _opposite_ or _next to_.**

1 The supermarket is _opposite_ the park.
2 The hospital is _____ the supermarket.
3 The cinema is _____ the post office and the café.
4 The church is _____ the café.
5 There's a bus stop _____ the cinema.
6 The cinema is _____ the post office.
7 The station is _____ the museum.
8 The hotel is _____ the hospital.

Listening

4 a ****** **1.24 Listen and write the places.**

b **1.24 Listen again and match the places to the directions.**

What places do people want?	What's the response?
1 _a bank_	a It's over there.
2 _____	b It's behind the cinema.
3 _____	c It's closed.
4 _____	d It's behind the church.
5 _____	e It's next to the station.
6 _____	f There's one in the next town.

c **Look at the chart. Write the dialogues.**

1 _Excuse me, is there a bank_ near here?
   Yes, there is. It's behind the cinema.
2 _____ in this town?
   _____
3 _____ near here?
   _____
4 _____ in this town?
   _____
5 _____ near here?
   _____
6 _____ near here?
   _____

Writing

5 ******* **Write about your town, or a town near you, and the things that are there.**

In my town there's a big square …

_____
_____
_____
_____
_____
_____

can / can't

1 ✴◼◼◼ **Look at the pictures and write sentences.**
Use *can* or *can't* and the phrases in the box.

| catch the ball   dance   draw   play the piano   play tennis   play volleyball   ride a bike   ski   spell   ~~swim~~ |

1 Tom _____can't swim._____

2 Isabel and Adam _____.

3 Samir _____.

4 Dylan and Morgan _____.

5 Bruce and Tess _____.

6 Jasmine _____.

7 Flora and Kate _____.

8 Rosa _____.

9 He _____.

10 The dog _____.

2 ✴✴◼◼ **Look at the pictures in exercise 1. Write questions and answers.**

1 _Can Tom swim? No, he can't._

2 _____

3 _____

4 _____

5 _____

6 _____

7 _____

8 _____

9 _____

10 _____

3 ✱✱ Write true sentences about yourself with *I can* or *I can't*.

'Hello, how are you?'

1 *I can speak English.* 2 _____ 3 _____ 4 _____

Write one more sentence about yourself.

5 _____ 6 _____ 7 _____ 8 _____

Listening

4 a ✱✱✱ 🎧 1.25 Listen and put a tick (✓) or cross (✗) on the poster.

BE A STAR FOR A DAY!
AT OUR TV STUDIOS.

What can you do?

SING? ✓
PLAY A MUSICAL INSTRUMENT?
PLAY THE GUITAR OR PIANO?
SPEAK FRENCH?
SPEAK SPANISH?
DANCE?
PLAY TENNIS OR BASKETBALL?
SWIM?
RUN LIKE THE WIND?

TELL US!

b Write sentences about Jessica.

1 *She can sing.*
2 _____
3 _____
4 _____
5 _____
6 _____
7 _____
8 _____
9 _____

c Look at the poster. What can or can't you do?

_____
_____
_____
_____
_____
_____

Progress check

1 Where are the books? Write sentences with *There's / There are*.

1. *There's a book* under *the bed* .
2. _____ behind _____ .
3. _____ between _____ .
4. _____ in front of _____ .
5. _____ next to _____ .
6. _____ in _____ .
7. _____ on _____ .

2 a Draw a picture of your bedroom.

[blank drawing box]

b Write sentences with *There's / There are*.

1. *There's a big wardrobe.* _____
2. *There are two chairs.* _____
3. _____
4. _____
5. _____
6. _____
7. _____
8. _____

3 Write the places in a town.

1. tntiosa — _station_
2. ainmec — _____
3. phsliaot — _____
4. hetarte — _____
5. eaurqs — _____
6. meumus — _____
7. isimgmwn lopo — _____
8. kanb — _____

4 🎧 1.26 Listen and label the places in the town.

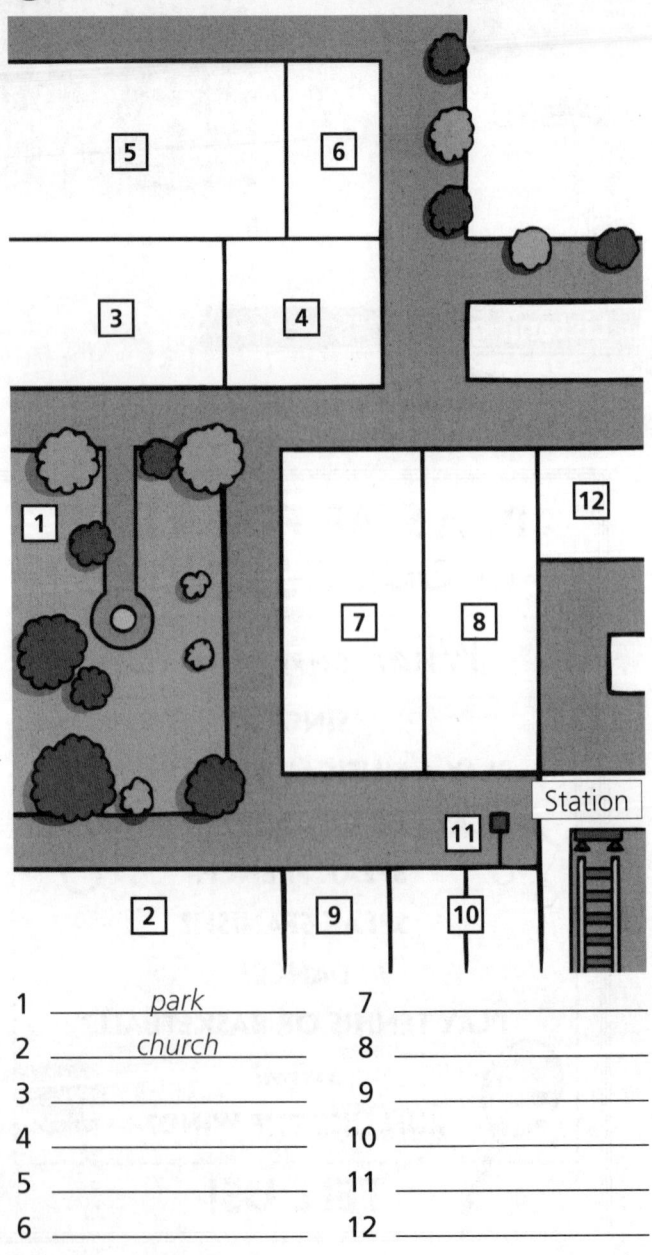

1. *park*   7. _____
2. *church*   8. _____
3. _____ 9. _____
4. _____ 10. _____
5. _____ 11. _____
6. _____ 12. _____

5 Now answer the questions about the town.

1 What is opposite the museum?
   The school is opposite the museum.

2 What is between the church and the bank?
   _____

3 Is there a theatre in the town?
   _____

4 What is between the church and the cafés?
   _____

5 What is opposite the hotel?
   _____

6 Is there a cinema in the town?
   _____

7 Are there two hotels?
   _____

8 What is in front of the supermarket?
   _____

6 Put the words in order to make questions (1–8). Find the answers (a–h).

1 Mr can speak Jones French ?
   Can Mr Jones speak French? ⬚ b

2 violin you the can play ?
   _____ ⬚

3 mother can your a game computer play ?
   _____ ⬚

4 dog can song your a sing ?
   _____ ⬚

5 Lily ride can bikes and Robbie ?
   _____ ⬚

6 bag heavy can this I carry ?
   _____ ⬚

7 find camera we the can ?
   _____ ⬚

8 run like Peter can wind the ?
   _____ ⬚

a No, it can't.   e Yes, you can.
b ~~Yes, he can.~~   f Yes, they can.
c No, she can't.   g Yes, I can.
d No, he can't.   h No, we can't.

I can ...

Write the answers and tick (✓) the correct box.

1 In my bedroom, there's
   a _____ next
   to the _____.
   There's a _____
   on the _____.

I can talk about houses and rooms.
   ⬚ Yes   ⬚ I need more practice

2 There _____ a hotel in
   our town. The hotel is
   _____ to the _____
   and _____ the post
   office.
   There _____ two cafés.
   The _____ is between the cafés.

I can talk about places in a town and say where they are.
   ⬚ Yes   ⬚ I need more practice

3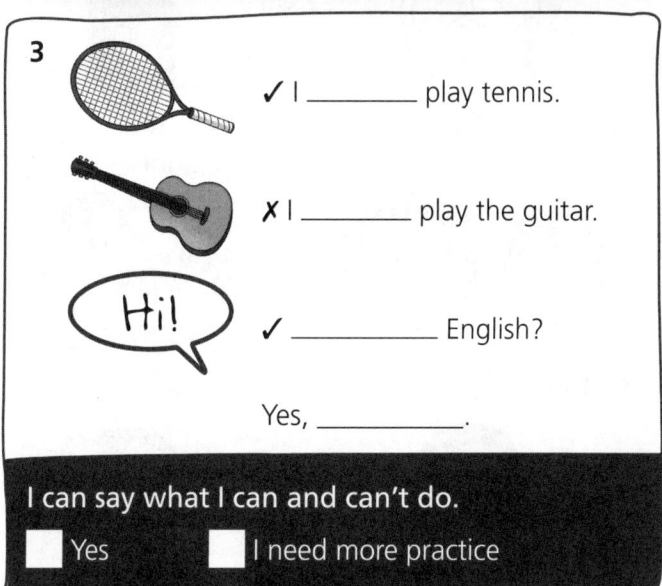
   ✓ I _____ play tennis.
   ✗ I _____ play the guitar.
   Hi!
   ✓ _____ English?
   Yes, _____.

I can say what I can and can't do.
   ⬚ Yes   ⬚ I need more practice

51

6 People

6A My friends

Describing people

1 ✱ **Label the pictures with the words in the box.**

bald   a beard   brown eyes   dark hair   fat   glasses
long hair   a moustache   short   short hair   slim   tall

1 He's _____ *fat.* _____   2 They're _____.

3 He's _____.   4 They're _____.

5 He's _____.   6 They've got _____.

7 He's got _____.   8 She's got _____.

9 They've got _____.   10 He's got _____.

11 She's got _____.   12 He's got _____.

2 ✱✱ 🎧 1.27 **Listen to Freddie describe his friend's family. Draw and colour the picture.**

Luke   Mr Green   Mrs Green   Sarah

3 ✱✱✱ **Describe the people.**

1 _This woman's got_
a long nose.
_____
_____
_____
_____

2 _This man's got_
a beard.
_____
_____
_____
_____

be or *have got*?

4 ✱ **Circle the correct words.**

1 He **'s** / **'s got** twelve years old.
2 I**'m** / **'ve got** a very big family.
3 I**'m** / **'ve got** tall and I**'m** / **'ve got** blue eyes.
4 My mother**'s** / **'s got** short hair.

5 Her eyes **are** / **have got** brown.
6 My brothers **are** / **have got** tall and they**'re** / **'ve got** fair hair.
7 Rachel**'s** / **'s got** tall and slim.
8 Jack**'s** / **'s got** quite short hair and he**'s** / **'s got** brown eyes.

have got / *has got*

5 ✱✱ **Read the text. What number are the people a–e?**

Mr Taylor is tall and slim. He's got a big moustache, but he hasn't got a beard. His wife is quite short and fat. She's got short fair hair. They've got three children. Their son, Charlie, isn't tall. He's got short dark hair and big brown eyes. Charlie's sister, Sophie, has got long fair hair and small blue eyes. Daisy Taylor is one year old. She hasn't got any hair or teeth. But she's got a big mouth!

a Mr Taylor _1_   b Mrs Taylor _____   c Charlie _____   d Sophie _____   e Daisy _____

6 ✱✱✱ **Write sentences.**

1 Emily _hasn't got long hair._
She _'s got short hair._

2 Leo _____.
He _____.

3 Josh _____.
He _____.

4 Ella and Bradley _____.
They _____.

5 Richard _____.
He _____.

6 Charlotte and Grace
_____.
They _____.

Writing

7 ✱✱✱ **Describe a person in your family. Then describe yourself. Use some of the words in the box to help you.**

> eyes   hair   quite / very – tall / short / fat / slim / bald   glasses   a beard   a moustache

_My ..._ _____
_____
_____
_____
_____
_____
_/ ..._ _____
_____
_____
_____
_____
_____

Present continuous

1 ✱◼◼◼ **Match the sentences to the pictures.**

1 [*Lucy and Anna are having dinner.*]

2 [*Dan is phoning a friend.*]

3 [*Jake and Erin are watching a DVD.*]

4 [*Ethan is buying clothes.*]

5 [*Dad is sitting on the sofa.*]

6 [*Ben and his friend are waiting for the train.*]

7 [*My sister is walking to the shops.*]

8 [*Mum is reading a book.*]

2 ✱✱◼◼ **Write what the people are doing.**

1 Alfie *'s lying in bed.*

2 Ryan _____.

3 Lola and Florence _____.

4 Jane _____.

5 Max and Frank _____.

6 Sanjay _____.

3 ★★★ **Look at the picture. Correct the sentences. Use the short forms.**

1 A man is eating lunch at the café.
   He isn't eating lunch. He's reading the newspaper.

2 A tall woman is listening to the radio in the park.
   She _____.

3 A man is reading a magazine at the bus stop.
   He _____.

4 Two boys are walking to the bus stop.
   They _____.

5 An old man is playing the violin.
   He _____.

6 Two girls are dancing in the park.
   They _____.

7 A bald man is getting in the car.
   He _____.

8 A young man and woman are sitting outside the café.
   They _____.

Listening

4 ★★ (🎧 1.28) **Listen and write the prices.**

1 *£6.50*   2 _____   3 _____

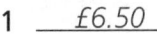 

4 _____   5 _____   6 _____

Shopping

5 ★★ **Put the dialogue in the correct order.**

And the poster? How much is that? ☐

Good morning! Can I help you? 1

Here you are. ☐

Yes. How much are the balloons, please? ☐

OK. Can I have three balloons and this poster, please? ☐

That's £8.75, then, please. ☐

Thank you. ☐

All the posters are £5.00 each. ☐

They're £1.25 each. ☐

6 ★★★ **What are the people saying? Write a dialogue.**

1 Adam   How much *is this magazine?*
   Assistant   _____.

2 Adam   _____?
   Assistant   _____.

3 Adam   _____ and this book, please?
   Assistant   Anything else?
   Adam   No, _____.

4 Assistant   _____.
   Adam   _____.
   Assistant   _____.

Present continuous

1 * Write the answers. Use the words in the box.

> Yes, they are.   No, they aren't.   No, we aren't.   ~~Yes, he is.~~
> Yes, she is.   Yes, he is.   No, she isn't.   No, it isnt.

1 Is he swimming?
Yes, he is.

2 Is she playing tennis?
_____

3 Are they listening to the radio? _____

4 Is he reading the newspaper?

_____

5 Are Maya and Tom drawing? _____

6 Is the dog running?
_____

7 Is Lydia having lunch?
_____

8 Are we going to the shops? _____

Listening

2 ** 🎧 1.29 **What are they doing now?**
Listen and label the picture with the names.

> Simon   Fatima   Tom and James   Ellen   Anna and Jo   Emma and Sophie   Adam   Katie   Jack and Ben

Present simple and present continuous

3 ★★ Write sentences with the present simple and the present continuous.

1 Tom usually rides a bike to school but today he *'s taking the bus.*

2 Maria usually _____ after school but today she _____.

3 Karl and Martin usually _____ after dinner but today they _____ music.

4 Tony usually _____ but today he _____.

5 Esme usually _____ to the park but today she _____.

6 Isaac and Harvey usually _____ at 4 o'clock but today they _____.

4 ★★★ Correct the sentences.

1 Mum is making dinner. She / talk / to her friend.
   Mum isn't making dinner. She's talking to her friend.

2 I'm reading a book. I / have / a shower.
   _____

3 William is going to the shops. He / go / to the cinema.
   _____

4 I have an apple for lunch every day. I / have / an orange.
   _____

5 Dad usually walks to work. He / usually / take / the train.
   _____

6 My friends are playing football in the garden. They / watch / TV.
   _____

7 We go to the park every weekend. We / take / the bus / to town.
   _____

Present simple or continuous?

5 ★★★ Put the verbs into the present simple or the present continuous.

Dear Carla

I am on holiday in a nice town in Spain. At the moment, I¹ *'m sitting* (sit) in my hotel room and I² _____ (write) to you! I³ _____ (look) at the hotel swimming pool – it's very big! Mum and Dad ⁴ _____ (watch) TV now and my sister Kate ⁵ _____ (listen) to music.
Every morning, we ⁶ _____ (go swimming) in the pool at 7.30, then we ⁷ _____ (have) breakfast at 8.15. After breakfast, I ⁸ _____ (play) tennis with my dad. Kate ⁹ _____ (go) to dance class with my mum – she ¹⁰ _____ (like) tennis!
¹¹ _____ you _____ (read) this postcard in your bedroom at home?
See you soon
Love
Emma

6D Clothes

Clothes

1 * Complete the crossword.

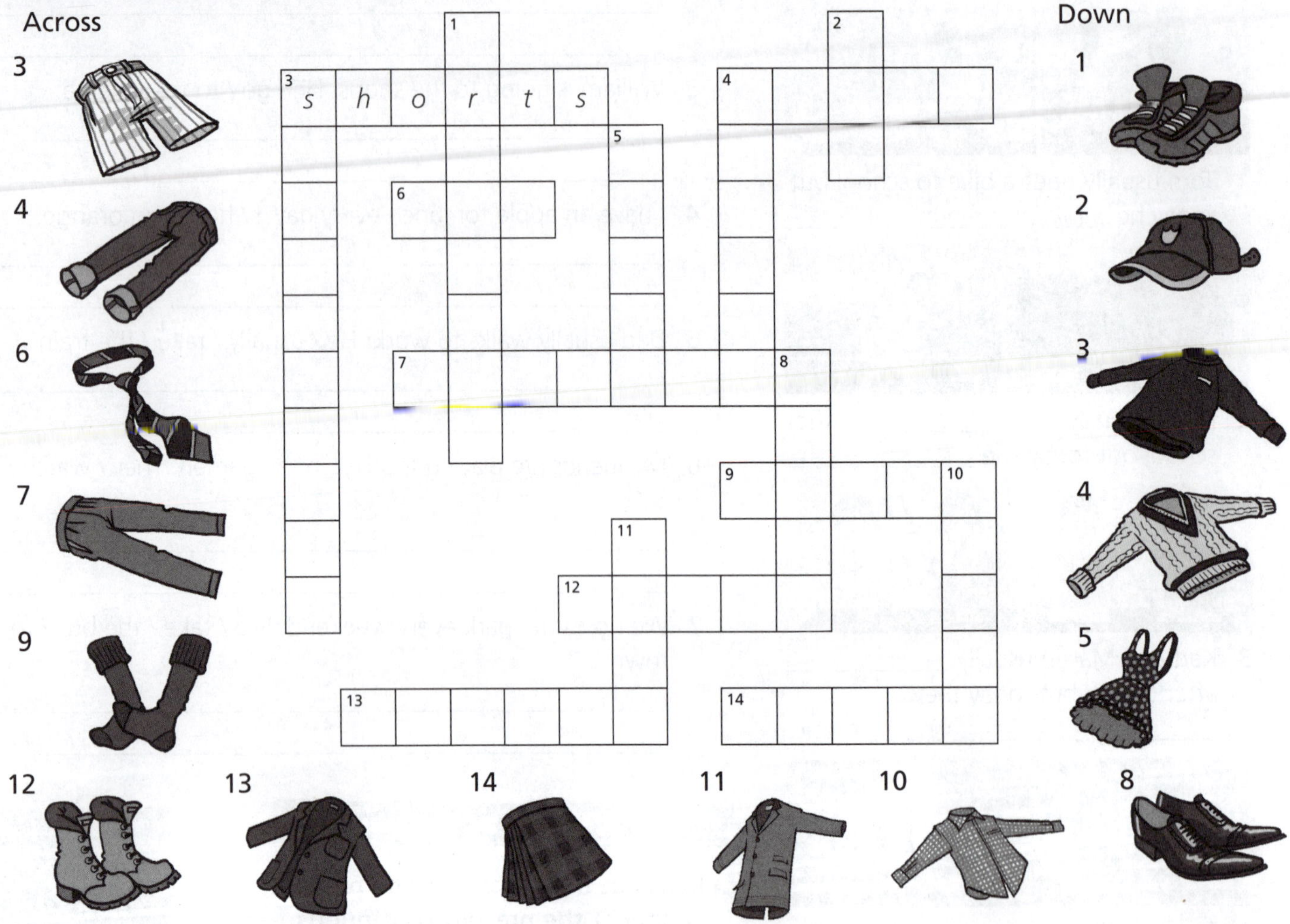

Across
3
4
6
7
9
Down
1
2
3
4
5
s h o r t s
12
13
14
11
10
8

2 ** What are they wearing? Colour the picture and write sentences.

1 The mother *'s wearing a blue dress.*

2 The father ______________________

____

______________________.

3 The boys ______________________

____

______________________.

4 The girl ______________________

____

______________________.

How much is / are?

3 ** Complete the dialogues.

1 **Customer** How much ___is this___ shirt?

 Assistant ___It's___ £19.99.

2 **Customer** How much _____ trainers?

 Assistant _____ £50.

3 **Customer** How much _____ cap?

 Assistant _____ £11.49.

4 **Customer** How much _____ boots?

 Assistant _____ £59.95.

5 **Customer** How much _____ tie?

 Assistant _____ £14.00.

6 **Customer** How much _____ jumper?

 Assistant _____ £24.99.

Writing

5 *** Answer the questions about yourself. Use the words in the box to help you.

> boots   a cap   a coat   a dress   a jacket   jeans
> a jumper   a shirt   shoes   shorts   a skirt
> a sweatshirt   a tie   trainers   trousers

What do you wear at school?

 ___I wear ..._____

_____

_____

_____

What are you wearing now?

_____

_____

_____

_____

Listening

4 a *** 🎧 1.30 Listen and colour Ben's clothes.

school

home

b 🎧 1.30 Listen again. Are the statements true (✓) or false (✗)?

1 Ben is twelve. ✓

2 Ben goes to a school in London. ☐

3 The girls at his school wear ties. ☐

4 The girls at his school wear blue skirts. ☐

5 Ben likes his uniform. ☐

6 Ben wears his favourite clothes at home. ☐

7 At the moment, he is sitting in the living room. ☐

8 He is sitting in an armchair. ☐

Progress check

1 **Describe the people. Use the words in the box.**

bald   a beard   dark (x2)   fair   long   a moustache   fat   short (x2)   slim (x3)   tall (x 2)

1 She _'s tall___ and __slim__. She's got short,
_____ hair.

2 He _____ and _____. He _____.
He _____ and _____.

3 He _____ and _____. He _____ hair.   **4** She _____ and _____. She _____ hair.

2 **Look at the pictures again. What are the people wearing?**

1 The girl _'s wearing a T-shirt___ and _____.
On her feet, _she's wearing socks_ and _____.

2 The man _____.
On his feet, _____.

3 The boy _____.
On his feet, _____.

4 The woman _____.
On her feet, _____.

3 Complete the dialogues. Put the verbs into the present simple or the present continuous.

Mrs Evans	Joel, can you go to the shops for me, please?
Joel	Oh, Mum, I¹ *'m watching* Football Weekly. (watch) I ²_____ it every week. (watch) Can Lily go?
Mrs Evans	No, she can't. She ³_____ her bedroom. (clean)
Mr Hall	Where's Belinda?
Mrs Hall	She ⁴_____ a shower. (have) She always ⁵_____ a shower in the morning. (have)
Steve	Where's Joe?
Abigail	He's in his bedroom. He ⁶_____ his homework. (do)
Steve	⁷_____ he ⁸_____ his homework every day? (do)
Abigail	No, he ⁹_____. He ¹⁰_____ it on Mondays, Wednesdays and Fridays. (do)

4 a 🎧 1.31 **Listen and write the prices of the clothes.**

1   *£17.99* ☑   2 _____ ☐

3 _____ ☐   4 _____ ☐

5 _____ ☐   6 _____ ☐

b 🎧 1.31 **Listen again. What do the people buy? Put a tick (✓) or a cross (✗).**

I can ...

Write the answers and tick (✓) the correct box.

1 Ian's tall and _____.

He _____ hair.

He _____ a _____ and _____.

He _____ a jacket, _____, _____ and _____.

I can describe people.

☐ Yes   ☐ I need more practice

2 I / usually / play tennis / Saturdays

today / go / to the swimming pool

_____, but today

_____.

We / sometimes / ride our bikes to school

today / take / the bus

We _____, but today

_____.

I can talk about routines, habits and what people are doing now.

☐ Yes   ☐ I need more practice

3 Assistant   Can _____ you?

You   How _____ T-shirts?

Assistant   _____ pounds each.

You   _____ the red T-shirt, please?

Assistant   That's 10 _____.   £10

I can ask for things in a shop and talk about how much they cost.

☐ Yes   ☐ I need more practice

Revision

1 Write sentences about the picture. Use *There's* / *There are*.

1 ___There's an apple___ on a desk.
2 _____ two oranges.
3 _____ on a desk.
4 _____ chairs.
5 _____ on the chair.
6 _____ in the school bag.
7 _____ picture on the _____.
8 _____ four people: two _____, a
   _____ and one _____. She's the
   teacher.

2 Complete the sentences with the correct forms of *be*. Use the short forms.

> My name [1]'s____ Jin. I [2]_____ from
> China. My Internet friend's name is Debbie.
> She [3]_____ from the USA. Debbie's
> grandparents [4]_____ from Italy. Debbie's
> brother's name [5]_____ Rob. He [6]_____
> eighteen. He [7]_____ a student.

3 Now answer the questions. Write the correct answers.

1 Is Jin from the USA?
   No, she isn't. She's from China.
2 Is her Internet friend from the USA?
   _____
3 Are Debbie's grandparents from the USA?
   _____
4 How old is Rob?
   _____
5 Is Rob a teacher?
   _____

4 Whose things are they? Write sentences.

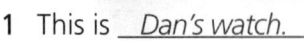 Dan

 Mr Lee

1 This is _Dan's watch._   2 This is _____
   _____.   _____.

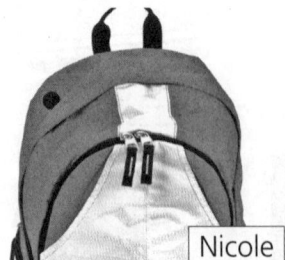 Nicole

 Jason

3 This is _____   4 This is _____
   _____.   _____.

 Ellie

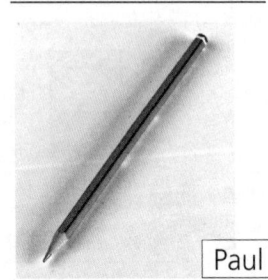 Paul

5 This is _____   6 This is _____
   _____.   _____.

5 What pets have they got? Write sentences.

Matilda

1 Matilda _____.

Joe

2 Joe _____.

Laura and Florence

3 Laura and Florence _____.

George

4 George _____.

6 Look at the pictures in exercise 5. Complete the dialogue.

Teacher Have you ¹___*got*___ a pet, George?
George   Yes, ²_____! ³_____ got a
⁴_____.
Teacher ⁵_____ your rabbit brown?
George   No, ⁶_____. It's ⁷_____.
Teacher ⁸_____ it small?
George   No, it's ⁹_____ and ¹⁰_____!
Teacher ¹¹_____ Laura and Florence
¹²_____ rabbits, too?
George   No, ¹³_____. They ¹⁴_____
two ¹⁵_____. They ¹⁶_____ brown
and white.

7 Write the opposites in the crossword.

Down
1 good
2 long
3 thick

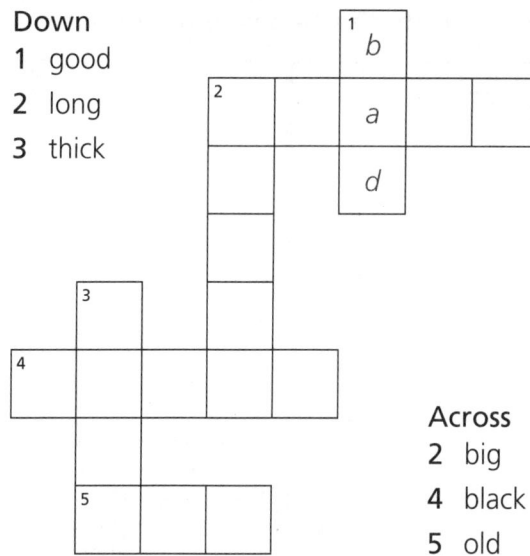

Across
2 big
4 black
5 old

8 What do they do at the weekend? Complete the sentences.

Ed	Annemarie

Ed ¹___*plays*___ tennis. He ²_____ TV and
³_____ to the radio. He ⁴_____ read
⁵_____. Annemarie ⁶_____ the guitar.
She ⁷_____ swimming, and she ⁸_____
her bike in the park.
Annemarie and Ed ⁹_____ to school at the
weekend, but they ¹⁰_____ their homework.

9 a 🔊 1.32 **Adam is talking about his flat. Listen and write the names of the rooms.**

1 _____ 2 _____

3 _____ 4 _____

b 🔊 1.32 **Listen again and draw the furniture in each room.**

10 Look at the picture. Complete the sentences with the correct prepositions.

1 The sink is ___behind___ the table.
2 The fridge is _____ the two cupboards.
3 The cooker is _____ the door.
4 The sink is _____ the window.
5 The fridge is _____ the cooker.
6 The small chair is _____ the table.

11 Complete the sentences with *can* or *can't*.

Can you …?	Jason	Sophie
swim	✓	✓
play a musical instrument	✗	✓
play football	✓	✗
play tennis	✗	✓
sing	✓	✓
dance	✗	✗

1 Jason and Sophie ___can___ swim.
2 Jason _____ play a musical instrument, but Sophie _____ play the piano.
3 Jason _____ play football, but he _____ play tennis.
4 Sophie _____ play football, but she _____ play tennis.
5 They _____ sing, but they _____ dance.

12 What are the people doing in the pictures? Use the verbs in the box.

read   listen   play   have   walk   ~~sit~~

1 The man *'s sitting* _____ in a café.
2 He _____ a book.
3 He _____ lunch.
4 The woman _____ in the park.
5 She _____ to her MP3 player.
6 Two boys _____ football.

Grammar summary

1 Introduction

1.1 Introductions

What's your name?	I'm Susan. My name's Tom.

We use *am* or *is* (the verb *be*) to describe someone or something.

a The short form of *is* is *'s*. The short form of *am* is *'m*. We often use the short forms when we speak.

b When we tell someone our name we can say *I'm* ... or *My name's* ...

(see also 1.2, 2.2, 2.3)

Translate
My name's ...
I'm ...

1.2 *my, your*

My name's Tom.
What's **your** name?
What's **your** phone number?

We use *my* and *your* for both male and female people. *Your* can be singular or plural.

Translate
My book is yellow.
Your bag is brown.

1.3 Articles: *a / an*

a pencil	an orange
a house	an apple
a desk	an umbrella

A / an is used to indicate that there is one of something.
When the following noun begins with a consonant sound we use *a*.
When the following noun begins with a vowel sound we use *an*.

Translate
a picture   a watch
an apple   an exercise book

1.4 Instructions

affirmative	negative
Talk.	**Don't** talk.
Sit down.	**Don't** sit down.

a To make affirmative instructions or commands we use the infinitive of the verb.

b To make the negative form we use *Don't* + the infinitive.

Translate
Close your book.
Don't look.
Draw a house.

1.5 Question words: *What ...?*

What's this? It's a watch.
What's your name? I'm Terry.
What's your phone number? It's 547210.

Translate
What's this?
It's a toothbrush.
What's your mobile number?

1.6a Regular plurals

We add *-s* to most singular nouns to show that there is more than one.

a desk   *two desks*
a boy   *two boys*

We add *-es* to some nouns which end in *-ch, -sh, -ss* or *-x*.

a box   *two boxes*
a glass   *two glasses*

1.6b Irregular plurals

These nouns are different in the plural form and do not take *-s*.

a man   *two men*
a woman   *two women*
a child   *two children*
a person   *two people*

1.7   There is / are ...

There's **a** cat.
There's **an** orange.
There **are** four glasses.

We can use *There is / are* when we want to show or describe something we can see. The short form of *There is* is *There's*.

Translate
There's a cat on the chair.
There are three dogs.

2   Friends and family

2.1   be: affirmative (long forms)

I	am	
We		
You	are	at home.
They		eleven.
He		from the USA.
She	is	
It		

You can be singular or plural, but the verb is the same for both.

Translate
I am from Greece.
You (plural) are in the classroom.
She is from the UK.

2.2   be: affirmative (short forms)

I am = **I'm**
He is = **He's**
She is = **She's**
It is = **It's**
We are = **We're**
You are = **You're**
They are = **They're**

We often use the short forms of the verb *be* when we speak.
We always use the long form after *this* and in *Yes / No* questions.
This is my brother.
Are you from America?

Translate
We're on holiday.
He's in Australia.
I'm in London.

2.3   be: negative

I	am not 'm not	
We		
You	are not aren't	at home.
They		eleven.
He		from the USA.
She	is not isn't	
It		

To make the negative long form we put *not* after the verb.
For the short form we use *'m not, isn't* or *aren't*.

Translate
I'm not from London.
He isn't in the classroom.
We aren't twelve.

2.4   Possessive adjectives

Subject	Possessive adjective	Noun (= thing possessed)
I	my	
you	your	
he	his	book
she	her	pen
it	its	house
we	our	name
they	their	

The possessive adjective relates to the subject, NOT the noun.
For men we use *his*. For women we use *her*.
His name is Duncan.   *Her* name is Maria.
For animals we use *its*, but you can also use *his / her* for pets.

Translate
His name is Tony.
Her name is Jane.
The dog is in its house.

2.5a Question words: *Whose ...?*

Whose book is this? It's Ben's book.

We use *Whose* to ask about the owner of something.

Translate
Whose watch is this?
It's Rebecca's watch.

2.5b Possessive *'s*

Tim**'s** house
Stephanie**'s** apple
The boy**'s** pencil

To show possession we put *'s* on the end of the noun.

Translate
Deborah's mobile
Tony's brother
The girl's bag

2.6 *be:* questions

Am	I	
Are	we you they	at home? in the classroom? from Britain?
Is	he she it	
Where is she from? **When** is your birthday?		

To make questions with the verb *be* we put the verb before the subject.

*He **is** our new classmate*   ***Is** he our new classmate?*

*They **are** in the garden.*   ***Are** they in the garden?*

For *Wh-* questions we add the question word at the beginning.

Translate
Is he friendly?
Are they singers?
Where are you from?

2.7 *be:* short answers

Are you from France?	**Yes, I am.**
Is she on the phone?	**No, she isn't.**

We always use the long form in affirmative short answers.
*Yes, we **are**. (NOT Yes, we're.)*
We can use short forms in negative short answers.

Translate
Are you sixteen? No, I'm not.
Are you eleven? Yes, I am.

2.8 Question words: *Who ...?*

Who's Oscar?	Oscar is a dog.
Who is the song for?	It's for my sister.

Translate
Who's your teacher?
Who is your friend?

2.9 Prepositions: *in, at, for*

Roger's	**in**	the garden.
Paul's	**at**	school.
This song is	**for**	you.

We use *at* when we talk about a place or building and *in* when we mean inside a place. We use *for* when we give something to someone.

Translate
Mrs Brown's in Paris.
Brian's at home.
This song is for my friends.

3 My world

3.1 *have got:* affirmative

I We You They	have 've	got	fifty books. two mp3 players. a mobile.
He She It	has 's		

Grammar Summary

We use *have got* to show possession. The short form of *have* is *'ve* and the short form of has is *'s*.

Translate
I've got three brothers.
She's got a computer.
We've got a dog.

3.2 *have got:* negative

I			
We	**have not**		fifty books.
You	**haven't**		two mp3
They		**got**	players.
He			a mobile.
She	**has not**		
It	**hasn't**		

To make *have got* negative, we put *not* after *have* or *has*. The short forms are *haven't got* and *hasn't got*.

Translate
We haven't got a brother.
He hasn't got a car.

3.3 *have got:* questions

Have	I we you they	**got**	a radio? a camera? a skateboard?
Has	he she it		
What has she **got** in her bag?			

To make a question with *have got* or *has got*, we put *have* or *has* in front of the subject. For *Wh-* questions we add the question word at the beginning.

Translate
Have you got a dog?
What DVDs have you got?
Has she got an MP3 player?

3.4a *have got:* affirmative short answers

	I we you they	have.
Yes,	he she it	has.

With short answers we use *have* or *has*, but NOT *got*.
Have you got a pen?
*Yes, I **have**.* (NOT *Yes, I have got.*)

Translate
Have they got a pet? Yes, they have.
Has she got a dog? Yes, she has.

3.4b *have got:* negative short answers

	I we you they	haven't.
No,	he she it	hasn't.

Translate
Has she got a house? No, she hasn't.
Have you got a brother? No, I haven't.

3.5 Adjectives

		adjective	noun
This is	a	yellow	pencil.
	an	orange	bag.
	a	new	mobile.
	an	old	picture.

Adjectives describe nouns. We put the adjective before the noun.

Translate
This is a white cat.
This is an orange watch.

3.6 favourite

What's your **favourite** day?
What are your **favourite** subjects?

We use *favourite* with the verb *be* to ask or talk about preferences.

Translate
What's your favourite band?
My favourite day is Saturday.

4 Time

4.1 Time

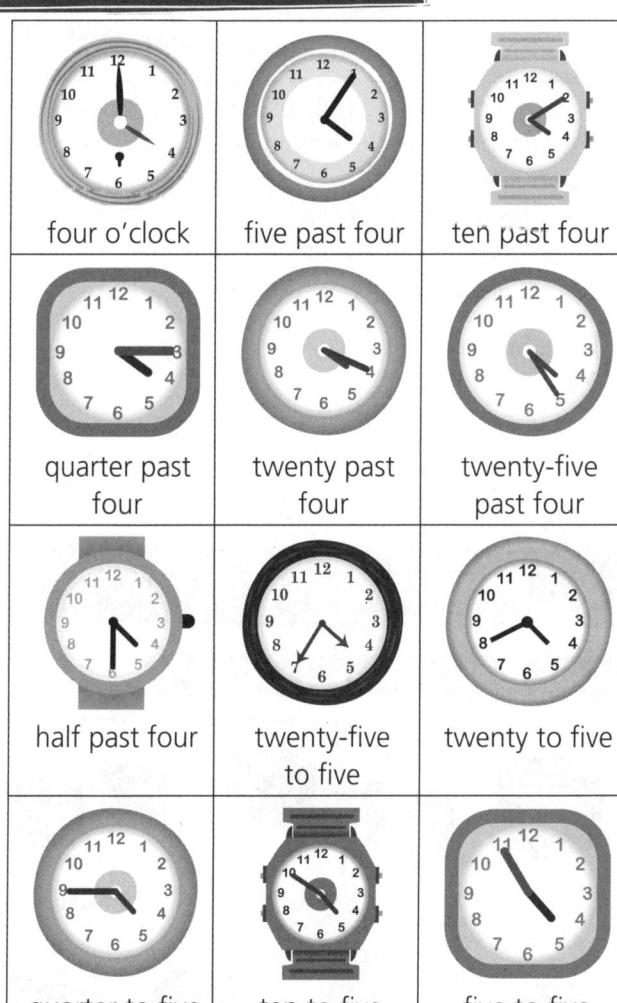

four o'clock	five past four	ten past four
quarter past four	twenty past four	twenty-five past four
half past four	twenty-five to five	twenty to five
quarter to five	ten to five	five to five

Translate
Half past nine
Ten o'clock
Quarter to eight

4.2 on + day / at + time

With days of the week we use *on*.
*I have Maths **on** Tuesdays.*

With times of day we use *at*.
*I get up **at** 8 o'clock.*

We often use *when* to ask about times.
When's the piano exam?

Translate
We have English on Tuesdays.
When's your History lesson?
He gets up at half past seven.

4.3 Present simple: affirmative

I We You They	**watch** TV after school. **play** the guitar. **collect** badges.
He She It	**likes** dogs. **plays** computer games. **starts** at three o'clock.

To make the present simple we use the infinitive.
For *he, she* and *it* we add *-s*.
There are some exceptions in spelling for the third person.

He She	**goes** to school. **does** her homework. **watches** television.

After *-o* and *-h*, we add *-es*.
We pronounce the *-es* /ɪz/ after *-ch*.

Translate
I collect badges.
She goes to school at eight o'clock.

4.4 Present simple: negative

I We You They	**don't**	get up at six. listen to music. play the drums. go to school. collect badges. watch TV.
He She It	**doesn't**	go to bed at nine. start at seven o'clock.

To form the negative of the present simple we use *don't / doesn't* and the infinitive.

The *-s* ending is now on *doesn't*, so we don't put an *-s* on the verb.

He plays tennis. He doesn't play tennis.

Translate

I don't like football.

She doesn't play the guitar.

We don't watch TV after school.

4.5 Present simple: questions

Do	I we you they	**play** football? **go** to school? **collect** badges?
Does	he she it	**get up** at six? **have** breakfast
When	do you does she do they	**start** school?

To make questions in the present simple we use *Do* or *Does* and the infinitive. For *Wh-* questions we add the question word at the beginning.

a We use *Do* for I, *you, we* and *they*.

They play tennis.
***Do** they play tennis?*
I get up at six.
*When **do** you get up?*

b We use *Does* for *he, she* and *it*. The *-s* ending is on *Does*, so we don't put an *-s* on the verb.

He watches TV after school.
***Does** he watch TV after school?*
He plays football on Saturday.
*When **does** he play football?*

4.6 Present simple: short answers

Yes,	I we you they	**do.**
	he she it	**does.**
No,	I we you they	**don't.**
	he she it	**doesn't.**

In short answers we only use *do / don't* or *does / doesn't*, but NOT the infinitive.

Do you like tea?
*Yes, I **do**. (NOT Yes, I like.)*
Does he work in a bank?
*No, he **doesn't**. (NOT No, he doesn't work.)*

Translate

Do they watch TV?

Yes, they do.

Does she work in a shop?

No, she doesn't.

5 Places

5.1 Prepositions of place

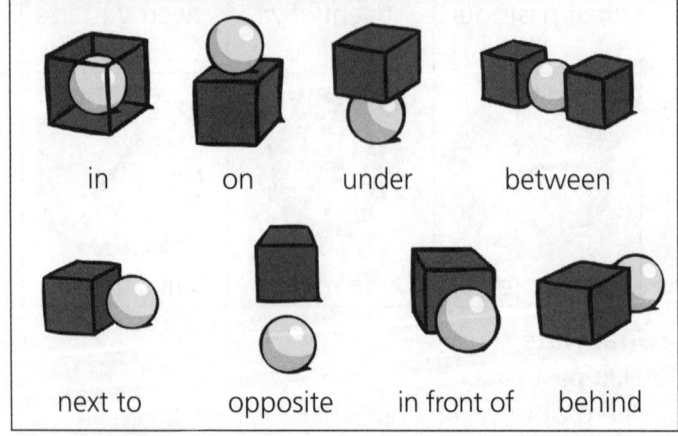

in   on   under   between

next to   opposite   in front of   behind

Prepositions of place tell us where something is.

a We use *in* with countries, towns, streets and rooms.

*They're on holiday **in** France.*
*There's a market **in** Witney.*
*You can buy CDs **in** Market Street.*
*I'm **in** the kitchen.*

b We use *in* with buildings when we want to say that we are inside the building, not outside.

*He's **in** the shop. (= He isn't in the street.)*
*He's **at** the shops. (= He's shopping.)*

Translate
The computer is in the box.
The cat is under the table.
The book is on the desk.
She's in Greece.
The station is between the bank and the school.
The library is next to my house.
He lives in High Street.

5.2 There is / are: affirmative and negative

There	is 's isn't	a dining room a cellar	in our house.
	are aren't	two bedrooms	

5.3a There is / are: questions

Is	there	a station a cinema	in your town?
Are		three churches a lot of shops	

5.3b There is / are: short answers

Is there a station in your town? **Yes, there is.**
Are there a lot of shops in your town? **Yes, there are.**

Translate
There are two cinemas in my town.
Is there a park near your school? Yes, there is.
Are there three bus stops in your town? Yes, there are.

5.4 can / can't

I We You They He She It	can can't	swim. dance. speak English.

We use *can* to talk about ability to do something.
Note that the third person does not have an *s*.
*He **can** swim. (*NOT *He cans swim.)*

5.5a can: questions

Can	I we you they he she it	spell your name? play tennis?

To make questions with *can*, we put *can* before the subject.
He can swim.
***Can** he swim?*

5.5b can: short answers

Can you speak French?	Yes, I can. No, he can't.

Translate
They can play the piano.
Can they ski? Yes, they can.
She can't speak French.
Can they dance? No, they can't.

5.6 Prepositions: to and at

*On Saturdays we go **to** the cinema. We're **at** the cinema.*

a We use *to* when there is movement.
b We use *at* when there is no movement.

Translate
I want to go to the shopping centre.
You can buy a drink at the café.

Grammar Summary

6 People

6.1 Present continuous: affirmative

I	am 'm	doing a project. playing the piano.
We You They	are 're	having a shower. making a poster.
He She It	is 's	watching TV. sitting in the car.

a We use the present continuous for actions that are happening now.

b We make the present continuous with be (am, is, are) and the present participle -ing.

c Note these spelling rules for the present participle:

1 with most verbs, add -ing.

read – reading
play – playing
do – doing

2 with verbs ending in -e, remove the -e and add -ing.

have – having
dance – dancing
write – writing

3 with verbs with a short vowel + one consonant, double the consonant and add -ing.

sit – sitting
get – getting

Translate

He's playing the piano.
They're sitting in the car.

6.2 Present continuous: negative

I	am not 'm not	playing the piano. skiing.
We You They	are not aren't	reading a book. watching TV. singing.
He She It	is not isn't	swimming. sitting in the car.

Translate

My friends aren't making a poster.
Cathy isn't driving to work.

6.3a Present continuous: questions

Am	I	speaking English?
Are	we you they	doing your homework? having a shower? writing an email?
Is	he she it	reading a magazine? going to school? listening to the radio?
Where is she going?		
What is he doing?		
Why are they talking?		

To make questions in the present continuous, we put *Am, Is* or *Are* in front of the subject. For *Wh*-questions add the question word at the beginning.

Translate

Are they going to the park?
What is your friend wearing?

6.3b Present continuous: short answers

Yes,	I	am.
	we you they	are.
	he she it	is.
No,	I'm	not.
	we you they	aren't.
	he she it	isn't.

In short answers we only use the verb *be*, NOT the present participle.

The verb *be* is in the full form in affirmative short answers.

Is she wearing jeans?

*Yes, she **is**. (NOT Yes, she is wearing.)*
Are you doing your homework?
*Yes, I **am**. (NOT Yes, I am doing.)*
Is he doing his homework?
*No, he **isn't**. (NOT No, he isn't doing.)*
Are you going home?
*No, I'**m not**. (NOT No, I'm not going.)*

Translate
Is he sitting in the car? Yes, he is.
Are they doing their homework? Yes, they are.
Are we going to the cinema? No, we aren't.

6.4 Present continuous and present simple

I **go** to school every day.
I **am going** to school now.
Tony **gets up** at eight o'clock every day.
It is eight o'clock now. Tony **is getting up**.

The present continuous is used for actions which are happening now. We often use it with words like *at the moment* and *now*.

*She **is doing** her homework **now**.*
*He **is reading** a book **at the moment**.*

The present simple is used for a regular action. It is often used with phrases like *every day, every morning, usually* or *all the time.*

*I **clean** my teeth **every morning**.*
*We **go** to school **every day**.*

Compare
*She **has** a shower **every day**.*
*She **is having** a shower **at the moment**.*

Translate
I play the piano every day.
I'm playing the piano at the moment.

6.5 How much is / are ...?

How much is this book?	It's £7.95.
How much are these DVDs?	They're £9.99 each.

We use *How much* to ask about the cost of something.

Translate
How much is this MP3 player?
How much are these jeans?

6.6 Clothes: singular and plural

My Your Her His Our Their	trousers jeans shorts	are	white. new. black.

Some names of clothes are always plural. They must have a plural verb.

Compare
*How much **is** this shirt? **It's** £15.*
*How much **are** these jeans? **They're** £20.*

Translate
My trousers are yellow.
Their shorts are new.

Wordlist

1 Introduction

1 A Hello
class /klɑːs/
dialogue /'daɪəlɒg/
different /'dɪfrənt/
expression /ɪk'spreʃn/
introduce /ɪntrə'djuːs/
partner /'pɑːtnə(r)/

Greetings / Introductions
Bye. /baɪ/
Good afternoon. /ˌgʊd ɑːftə'nuːn/
Goodbye. /gʊd'baɪ/
Good evening. /ˌgʊd 'iːvnɪŋ/
Good morning. /ˌgʊd 'mɔːnɪŋ/
Good night. /ˌgʊd 'naɪt/
Hello. /hə'ləʊ/
Hi! /haɪ/
How are you? /ˌhaʊ ə 'juː/
I'm ... /aɪm/
I'm fine, thanks. /ˌaɪm 'faɪn ˌθæŋks/
It's ... /ɪts/
My name's ... /'maɪ ˌneɪmz '.../
See you (later). /ˌsiː ˌjuː 'leɪtə(r)/
What's your name? /ˌwɒts ˌjɔː 'neɪm/
Who's this? /ˌhuːz 'ðɪs/

1 B In the classroom
a / an /ə, ən/
apple /'æpl/
bag /bæg/
board /bɔːd/
book /bʊk/
boy /bɔɪ/
but /bʌt, bət/
cat /kæt/
chair /tʃeə(r)/
desk /desk/
dog /dɒg/
door /dɔː(r)/
exercise book /'eksəsaɪz ˌbʊk/
girl /gɜːl/
house /haʊs/
It's a / an ... /'ɪts ə, ən/
label /'leɪbl/
man /mæn/
orange /'ɒrɪndʒ/
pen /pen/
pencil /'pensl/
picture /'pɪktʃə(r)/
umbrella /ʌm'brelə/
watch /wɒtʃ/
What's this? /ˌwɒts 'ðɪs/
Why ... ? /waɪ/
window /'wɪndəʊ/
woman /'wʊmən/

Instructions
Close your exercise book. /'kləʊz jər 'eksəsaɪz ˌbʊk/
Come here. /ˌkʌm 'hɪə(r)/
Don't listen. /'dəʊnt ˌlɪsn/
Draw. /drɔː/
Give me your book, please. /'gɪv ˌmiː ˌjɔː 'bʊk ˌpliːz/
Go to the board. /'gəʊ tə ðə ˌbɔːd/
Listen. /'lɪsn/
Look at the picture. /'lʊk ət ðə ˌpɪktʃə(r)/
Open your exercise book. /'əʊpən jər 'eksəsaɪz ˌbʊk /

Pick up your pencil. /'pɪk ʌp jə ˌpensl/
Put down your pencil. /'pʊt daʊn jə ˌpensl/
Read. /riːd/
Say 'Good morning'. /'seɪ ˌgʊd 'mɔːnɪŋ/
Sit down. /ˌsɪt 'daʊn/
Stand up. /ˌstænd 'ʌp/
Write on the board. /'raɪt ɒn ðə ˌbɔːd/

1 C Numbers
at /æt, ət/
Be careful! /ˌbi 'keəfl/
bone /bəʊn/
come /kʌm/
collect /kə'lekt/
continue /kən'tɪnjuː/
double /'dʌbl/
down /daʊn/
gate /geɪt/
give /gɪv/
heaven /'hevn/
hive /haɪv/
home /həʊm/
mine /maɪn/
my /maɪ/
number /'nʌmbə(r)/
old /əʊld/
on /ɒn/
phone number /'fəʊn ˌnʌmbə(r)/
play /pleɪ/
roll /rəʊl/
shoe /ʃuː/
some /sʌm, səm/
stick /stɪk/
this /ðɪs/
tree /triː/
up /ʌp/
What's your mobile number? /ˌwɒts ˌjɔː 'məʊbaɪl ˌnʌmbə(r)/
What's your phone number? /ˌwɒts ˌjɔː 'fəʊn ˌnʌmbə(r)/
What's your telephone number? /ˌwɒts ˌjɔː 'telɪfəʊn ˌnʌmbə(r)/
with /wɪð/

Numbers
oh (zero) /əʊ ('zɪərəʊ)/
one /wʌn/
two /tuː/
three /θriː/
four /fɔː(r)/
five /faɪv/
six /sɪks/
seven /'sevn/
eight /eɪt/
nine /naɪn/
ten /ten/
eleven /ɪ'levn/
twelve /twelv/
thirteen /θɜː'tiːn/
fourteen /fɔː'tiːn/
fifteen /fɪf'tiːn/
sixteen /sɪks'tiːn/
seventeen /sevn'tiːn/
eighteen /eɪ'tiːn/
nineteen /naɪn'tiːn/
twenty /'twenti/
twenty-one /ˌtwenti 'wʌn/
thirty /'θɜːti/
forty /'fɔːti/
fifty /'fɪfti/
sixty /'sɪksti/

seventy /'sevnti/
eighty /'eɪti/
ninety /'naɪnti/
a / one hundred /ə, ˌwʌn 'hʌndrəd/

1 D How do you spell that?
alphabet /'ælfəbet/
box /bɒks/
boxes /'bɒksɪz/
car /kɑː(r)/
child /tʃaɪld/
children /'tʃɪldrən/
column /'kɒləm/
glass /glɑːs/
glasses /'glɑːsɪz/
How do you spell ... ? /'haʊ də jə ˌspel '.../
letter /'letə(r)/
Let's ... /lets/
me /miː/
men /men/
only /'əʊnli/
oranges /'ɒrɪndʒɪz/
people /'piːpl/
person /'pɜːsn/
plural /'plʊərəl/
singular /'sɪŋgjələ(r)/
table /'teɪbl/
There's / There are ... /ðeəz, 'ðeər ɑː, ə/
toothbrush /'tuːθbrʌʃ/
toothbrushes /'tuːθbrʌʃɪz/
watches /'wɒtʃɪz/
women /'wɪmɪn/

Culture
actually /'æktʃuəli/
a lot of /ə 'lɒt əv/
call /kɔːl/
copy /'kɒpi/
country /'kʌntri/
dad /dæd/
English /'ɪŋglɪʃ/
everyone /'evriwʌn/
first name /'fɜːst ˌneɪm/
friend /frend/
from /frɒm, frəm/
full name /ˌfʊl 'neɪm/
have /hæv/
initials /ɪ'nɪʃlz/
it isn't /ˌɪt 'ɪznt/
middle name /'mɪdl ˌneɪm/
most /məʊst/
nickname /'nɪkneɪm/
often /'ɒfn, 'ɒftən/
only /'əʊnli/
parents /'peərənts/
real name /'rɪəl ˌneɪm/
short for /'ʃɔːt ˌfɔː(r), fə(r)/
short form /'ʃɔːt ˌfɔːm/
so /səʊ/
surname /'sɜːneɪm/
teacher /'tiːtʃə(r)/
that's ... /ðæts/
This is ... /'ðɪs ˌɪz/
too /tuː/
use (v) /juːz/

English Across the Curriculum
blue /bluː/
dart /dɑːt/
divided by /dɪ'vaɪdɪd ˌbaɪ/
equals /'iːkwəlz/

go from ... to ... and back   /ˌgəʊ frəm '... tə
   '... ən ˌbæk/
green   /griːn/
How far is it?   /ˌhaʊ 'fɑːr ˌɪz ˌɪt/
km   /ˌkeɪ 'em, 'kɪləmiːtəz, kɪ'lɒmɪtəz/
Maths   /mæθs/
minus   /'maɪnəs/
plus   /plʌs/
score   /skɔː(r)/
sum   /sʌm/
symbol   /'sɪmbl/
times   /taɪmz/
What's ... ?   /wɒts/
winner   /'wɪnə(r)/
yellow   /'jeləʊ/

Your Project

about   /ə'baʊt/
bed   /bed/
best friend   /ˌbest 'frend/
bike   /baɪk/
caption   /'kæpʃn/
computer   /kəm'pjuːtə(r)/
fall out   /ˌfɔːl 'aʊt/
favourite   /'feɪvərɪt/
find   /faɪnd/
football team   /'fʊtbɔːl ˌtiːm/
in   /ɪn/
life   /laɪf/
little   /'lɪtl/
make   /meɪk/
none   /nʌn/
no one   /'nəʊ ˌwʌn/
poster   /'pəʊstə(r)/
present (v)   /prɪ'zent/
project   /'prɒdʒekt/
put   /pʊt/
roll over   /ˌrəʊl 'əʊvə(r)/
say   /seɪ/
skateboard   /'skeɪtbɔːd/
speech bubble   /'spiːtʃ ˌbʌbl/
There were ...   /'ðeə wə(r)/
thing   /θɪŋ/
together   /tə'geðə(r)/

2 Friends and family

2 A Where are you from?

classroom   /'klɑːsruːm/
He isn't from ...   /ˌhiː 'ɪznt frəm/
I'm from ...   /'aɪm frəm/
I'm not from ...   /ˌaɪm 'nɒt frəm/
Internet friends   /'ɪntənet ˌfrendz/
She's from ...   /'ʃiːz frəm/
These are ...   /'ðiːz ə/
They're from ...   /'ðeə frəm/
We aren't from ...   /ˌwiː 'ɑːnt frəm/
We're from ...   /'wɪə frəm/
Who are ... ?   /'huː ə/
Where are they from?   /'weər ə ˌðeɪ 'frɒm/

Countries and cities

Australia   /ɒ'streɪliə/
Beijing   /beɪ'ʒɪŋ/
Brazil   /brə'zɪl/
Britain   /'brɪtn/
China   /'tʃaɪnə/
France   /frɑːns/
Germany   /'dʒɜːməni/
Greece   /griːs/
Italy   /'ɪtəli/
Japan   /dʒə'pæn/
London   /'lʌndən/
Milan   /mɪ'læn/

Moscow   /'mɒskəʊ/
New York   /ˌnjuː 'jɔːk/
Paris   /'pærɪs/
Rio de Janeiro   /ˌriːəʊ də ʒə'nɪərəʊ/
Russia   /'rʌʃə/
Sydney   /'sɪdni/
Spain   /speɪn/
the USA   /ðə ˌjuː ˌes 'eɪ/
Tokyo   /'təʊkiəʊ/

2 B My family

connect   /kə'nekt/
family   /'fæməli/
garden   /'gɑːdn/
mobile   /'məʊbaɪl/
photo   /'fəʊtəʊ/
Where is a / are ... ?   /'weər ˌɪz ə, ˌɑː(r),
   ə(r)/
Whose ... is this?   /ˌhuːz '... ɪz ˌðɪs/

Family

aunt   /ɑːnt/
brother   /'brʌðə(r)/
cousin   /'kʌzn/
daughter   /'dɔːtə(r)/
father   /'fɑːðə(r)/
grandchildren   /'græntʃɪldrən/
grandfather / granddad   /'grænfɑːðə(r),
   'grændæd/
grandmother / grandma   /'grænmʌðə(r),
   'grænmɑː/
grandparents   /'grænpeərənts/
mother (mum)   /'mʌðə(r), mʌm/
sister   /'sɪstə(r)/
son   /sʌn/
uncle   /'ʌŋkl/

Possessive adjectives

her   /hɜː(r)/
his   /hɪz/
its   /ɪts/
our   /ɑː(r), 'aʊə(r)/
their   /ðeə(r)/
your   /jɔː(r)/

2 C Mickey, Millie and Mut

alive   /ə'laɪv/
Are they ... ?   /ˌɑː ˌðeɪ '.../
Are you ... ?   /ˌɑː ˌjuː '.../
avenue   /'ævənjuː/
classmate   /'klɑːsmeɪt/
dead   /ded/
Excuse me.   /ɪk'skjuːz ˌmiː/
film star   /'fɪlm ˌstɑː(r)/
friendly   /'frendli/
growl   /graʊl/
Is this ... ?   /ˌɪz ˌðɪs '.../
Melbourne   /'melbɔːn/
neighbour   /'neɪbə(r)/
new   /njuː/
no   /nəʊ/
not   /nɒt/
over there   /ˌəʊvə 'ðeə(r)/
Pleased to meet you.   /ˌpliːzd tə 'miːt ˌjuː/
policeman   /pə'liːsmən/
postman   /'pəʊstmən/
road   /rəʊd/
singer   /'sɪŋə(r)/
sportsperson   /'spɔːtspɜːsn/
student   /'stjuːdnt/
Thank you.   /'θæŋk ˌjuː/
very   /'veri/
yes   /jes/

2 D What day is it today?

at home   /ət 'həʊm/
at the shops   /ət ðə 'ʃɒps/
birthday   /'bɜːθdeɪ/
caller   /'kɔːlə(r)/
chart   /tʃɑːt/
days of the week   /ˌdeɪz əv ðə 'wiːk/
DJ   /'diː ˌdʒeɪ/
for   /fɔː(r), fə(r)/
Happy birthday.   /ˌhæpi 'bɜːθdeɪ/
How old are you?   /'haʊ ˌəʊld ə ˌjuː/
How old is he?   /'haʊ ˌəʊld ˌɪz ˌhiː/
OK   /ˌəʊ 'keɪ/
record (n)   /'rekɔːd/
show   /ʃəʊ/
song   /sɒŋ/
text   /tekst/
today   /tə'deɪ/
week   /wiːk/
What is ... ?   /ˌwɒt ɪz '.../
When is his birthday?   /ˌwen ˌɪz ˌhɪz
   'bɜːθdeɪ/
Whose is ... ?   /ˌhuːz ɪz '.../

Days of the week

Monday   /'mʌndeɪ/
Tuesday   /'tjuːzdeɪ/
Wednesday   /'wenzdeɪ/
Thursday   /'θɜːzdeɪ/
Friday   /'fraɪdeɪ/
Saturday   /'sætədeɪ/
Sunday   /'sʌndeɪ/

Culture

address   /ə'dres/
album   /'ælbəm/
bank   /bæŋk/
big   /bɪg/
British   /'brɪtɪʃ/
city   /'sɪti/
crossing   /'krɒsɪŋ/
detective   /dɪ'tektɪv/
famous   /'feɪməs/
house number   /'haʊs ˌnʌmbə(r)/
just   /dʒʌst/
know   /nəʊ/
Liverpool   /'lɪvəpuːl/
outside   /aʊt'saɪd/
place   /pleɪs/
postcode   /'pəʊstkəʊd/
Prime Minister   /ˌpraɪm 'mɪnɪstə(r)/
real   /rɪəl, 'riːəl/
recording studio   /rɪ'kɔːdɪŋ ˌstjuːdiəʊ/
room   /ruːm/
street   /striːt/
town   /taʊn/
webcam   /'webkæm/

English Across the Curriculum

between   /bɪ'twiːn/
cold   /kəʊld/
continent   /'kɒntɪnənt/
desert   /'dezət/
Geography   /dʒi'ɒgrəfi/
map   /mæp/
mountain   /'maʊntən/
mountain range   /'maʊntən ˌreɪndʒ/
next to   /'nekst tə/
ocean   /'əʊʃn/
point   /pɔɪnt/
river   /'rɪvə(r)/
world   /wɜːld/

Geographical places

Africa /ˈæfrɪkə/
Amazon River /ˌæməzən ˈrɪvə(r)/
Antarctica /ænˈtɑːktɪkə/
Asia /ˈeɪʒə/
Europe /ˈjʊərəp/
Himalayas /hɪməˈleɪəz/
Nile River /ˌnaɪl ˈrɪvə(r)/
North America /ˌnɔːθ əˈmerɪkə/
Oceania /ˌəʊsiˈɑːniə/
Rocky Mountains /ˌrɒki ˈmaʊntənz/
Sahara Desert /səˌhɑːrə ˈdezət/
South America /ˌsaʊθ əˈmerɪkə/

Oceans

Arctic Ocean /ˌɑːktɪk ˈəʊʃn/
Atlantic Ocean /ətˌlæntɪk ˈəʊʃn/
Indian Ocean /ˌɪndiən ˈəʊʃn/
Pacific Ocean /pəˌsɪfɪk ˈəʊʃn/

Revision

black /blæk/
card /kɑːd/
cue /kjuː/
family tree /ˌfæməli ˈtriː/

Your Project

bring back /ˌbrɪŋ ˈbæk/
drawing /ˈdrɔːɪŋ/
interview /ˈɪntəvjuː/
over /ˈəʊvə(r)/
plan /plæn/
sea /siː/
title /ˈtaɪtl/

3 My world

3 A I've got a computer

bedroom /ˈbedruːm/
good /ɡʊd/
have (got) /ˌhæv (ˈɡɒt)/
living room /ˈlɪvɪŋ ˌruːm/
lucky /ˈlʌki/

Possessions

camera /ˈkæmərə/
computer game /kəmˈpjuːtə ˌɡeɪm/
DVD player /ˌdiː ˌviː ˈdiː ˌpleɪə(r)/
games console /ˈɡeɪmz ˌkɒnsəʊl/
MP3 player /ˌem ˌpiː ˈθriː ˌpleɪə(r)/
radio /ˈreɪdiəʊ/
remote-controlled car /rɪˌməʊt kənˌtrəʊld ˈkɑː(r)/
television /ˈtelɪvɪʒn/

3 B Mut's present

act /ækt/
basket /ˈbɑːskɪt/
ball /bɔːl/
blanket /ˈblæŋkɪt/
cap /kæp/
cover /ˈkʌvə(r)/
cricket bat /ˈkrɪkɪt ˌbæt/
describe /dɪˈskraɪb/
difference /ˈdɪfrəns/
jumper /ˈdʒʌmpə(r)/
mouth /maʊθ/
nice /naɪs/
now /naʊ/
present (n) /ˈpreznt/
Really? /ˈrɪəli, ˈriːəli/
school /skuːl/
small /smɔːl/
these /ðiːz/
T-shirt /ˈtiː ˌʃɜːt/

Colours

brown /braʊn/
grey /ɡreɪ/
red /red/
white /waɪt/

Other adjectives

bad /bæd/
long /lɒŋ/
short /ʃɔːt/
thick /θɪk/
thin /θɪn/

3 C Have you got a pet?

animal /ˈænɪml/
asleep /əˈsliːp/
band /bænd/
beautiful /ˈbjuːtɪfl/
beginning with ... /bɪˈɡɪnɪŋ ˌwɪð/
boring /ˈbɔːrɪŋ/
pet /pet/
tail /teɪl/
What kind of ... is it? /ˌwɒt ˌkaɪnd əv ˈ... ˌɪz ˌɪt/

Pets

bird /bɜːd/
budgie /ˈbʌdʒi/
fish /fɪʃ/
hamster /ˈhæmstə(r)/
horse /hɔːs/
mice /maɪs/
mouse /maʊs/
parrot /ˈpærət/
rabbit /ˈræbɪt/
rat /ræt/
snake /sneɪk/
spider /ˈspaɪdə(r)/

3 D My school

afternoon /ɑːftəˈnuːn/
assembly /əˈsembli/
break /breɪk/
compare /kəmˈpeə(r)/
each /iːtʃ/
good at /ˈɡʊd ˌæt, ət/
great /ɡreɪt/
last /lɑːst/
lesson /ˈlesn/
lunch /lʌntʃ/
next /nekst/
registration /redʒɪˈstreɪʃn/
subject /ˈsʌbdʒɪkt/
term /tɜːm/
timetable /ˈtaɪmteɪbl/
uniform /ˈjuːnɪfɔːm/
wear /weə(r)/
year /jɪə(r)/

School subjects

Art and Design /ˌɑːt ən dɪˈzaɪn/
Biology /baɪˈɒlədʒi/
Chemistry /ˈkemɪstri/
Citizenship /ˈsɪtɪzənʃɪp/
Design and Technology /dɪˌzaɪn ən tekˈnɒlədʒi/
French /frentʃ/
History /ˈhɪstri/
ICT (Information and Communication Technology) /ˌaɪ ˌsiː ˈtiː, ˌɪnfəˌmeɪʃn ən kəˌmjuːnɪˌkeɪʃn tekˈnɒlədʒi/
Music /ˈmjuːzɪk/
PE (Physical Education) /ˌpiː ˈiː, ˌfɪzɪkl edʒuˈkeɪʃn/
Physics /ˈfɪzɪks/

RE (Religious Education) /ˌɑːr ˈiː, rɪˌlɪdʒəs edʒuˈkeɪʃn/
Science /ˈsaɪəns/

Culture

about /əˈbaʊt/
England /ˈɪŋɡlənd/
from ... to ... /frəm ˌ... tə ˈ.../
half /hɑːf/
morning /ˈmɔːnɪŋ/
packed lunch /ˌpækt ˈlʌntʃ/
primary school /ˈpraɪməri ˌskuːl/
pupil /ˈpjuːpl/
sandwich /ˈsænwɪtʃ/
school day /ˈskuːl ˌdeɪ/
school system /ˈskuːl ˌsɪstəm/
secondary school /ˈsekəndri ˌskuːl/
sixth form /ˈsɪksθ ˌfɔːm/
sports match /ˈspɔːts ˌmætʃ/
Wales /weɪlz/

English Across the Curriculum

human /ˈhjuːmən/
touch /tʌtʃ/

Parts of an animal's body

arm /ɑːm/
beak /biːk/
body /ˈbɒdi/
ear /ɪə(r)/
eye /aɪ/
feathers /ˈfeðəz/
foot /fʊt/
fur /fɜː(r)/
hand /hænd/
head /hed/
leg /leɡ/
nose /nəʊz/
teeth /tiːθ/
whiskers /ˈwɪskəz/
wing /wɪŋ/

Revision

adjective /ˈædʒɪktɪv/
hair /heə(r)/
possessions /pəˈzeʃnz/

Your Project

chorus /ˈkɔːrəs/
day /deɪ/
Games /ɡeɪmz/

4 Time

4 A What's the time, please?

activity /ækˈtɪvəti/
birthday party /ˈbɜːθdeɪ ˌpɑːti/
clock /klɒk/
concert /ˈkɒnsət/
dance /dɑːns/
exam /ɪɡˈzæm/
game /ɡeɪm/
half past /ˈhɑːf ˌpɑːst/
hockey /ˈhɒki/
match /mætʃ/
o'clock /əˈklɒk/
party /ˈpɑːti/
past /pɑːst/
piano /piˈænəʊ/
punctuation /ˌpʌŋktʃuˈeɪʃn/
quarter past /ˈkwɔːtə ˌpɑːst/
quarter to /ˈkwɔːtə tə/
tennis /ˈtenɪs/
time /taɪm/

to   /tuː, tə/
volleyball   /ˈvɒlibɔːl/
What's the time?   /ˌwɒts ðə ˈtaɪm/

4 B My day

after   /ˈɑːftə(r)/
arrive at school   /əˌraɪv ət ˈskuːl/
at the weekend   /ət ðə wiːkˈend/
before   /bɪˈfɔː(r)/
breakfast   /ˈbrekfəst/
brush your teeth   /ˌbrʌʃ ˌjɔː ˈtiːθ/
bus   /bʌs/
coat   /kəʊt/
dinner   /ˈdɪnə(r)/
do your homework   /ˌduː ˌjɔː ˈhəʊmwɜːk/
finish   /ˈfɪnɪʃ/
get up   /ˌget ˈʌp/
go home   /ˌgəʊ ˈhəʊm/
go on the Internet   /ˌgəʊ ˌɒn ði ˈɪntənet/
go to bed   /ˌgəʊ tə ˈbed/
go to school   /ˌgəʊ tə ˈskuːl/
go to sleep   /ˌgəʊ tə ˈsliːp/
go to work   /ˌgəʊ tə ˈwɜːk/
half an hour   /ˈhɑːf ən ˌaʊə(r)/
have a shower   /ˌhæv ə ˈʃaʊə(r)/
have breakfast   /ˌhæv ˈbrekfəst/
have dinner   /ˌhæv ˈdɪnə(r)/
have lunch   /ˌhæv ˈlʌntʃ/
homework   /ˈhəʊmwɜːk/
in bed   /ˌɪn ˈbed/
Internet exchange   /ˈɪntənet ɪks,tʃeɪndʒ/
kitchen   /ˈkɪtʃɪn/
listen to music   /ˌlɪsn tə ˈmjuːzɪk/
listen to the radio   /ˌlɪsn tə ðə ˈreɪdiəʊ/
magazine   /ˌmægəˈziːn/
or   /ɔː(r)/
put on   /ˌpʊt ˈɒn/
school bus   /ˈskuːl ˌbʌs/
start   /stɑːt/
take the bus   /ˌteɪk ðə ˈbʌs/
take the train   /ˌteɪk ðə ˈtreɪn/
talk about   /ˈtɔːk əˌbaʊt/
TV   /ˌtiː ˈviː/
typical   /ˈtɪpɪkl/
walk   /wɔːk/
watch TV   /ˌwɒtʃ ˌtiː ˈviː/

4 C Free time

badge   /bædʒ/
comic   /ˈkɒmɪk/
football card   /ˈfʊtbɔːl ˌkɑːd/
free time   /ˌfriː ˈtaɪm/
go skiing   /ˌgəʊ ˈskiːɪŋ/
go swimming   /ˌgəʊ ˈswɪmɪŋ/
happen   /ˈhæpən/
like   /laɪk/
paragraph   /ˈpærəɡrɑːf/
play a musical instrument   /ˌpleɪ ə
   ˌmjuːzɪkl ˈɪnstrəmənt/
play computer games   /ˌpleɪ kəmˈpjuːtə
   ˌgeɪmz/
play football   /ˌpleɪ ˈfʊtbɔːl/
play ice hockey   /ˌpleɪ ˈaɪs ˌhɒki/
play tennis   /ˌpleɪ ˈtenɪs/
play the guitar   /ˌpleɪ ðə ɡɪˈtɑː(r)/
play the piano   /ˌpleɪ ðə piˈænəʊ/
play the violin   /ˌpleɪ ðə vaɪəˈlɪn/
Slovakia   /sləˈvækiə/
sport   /spɔːt/
sports centre   /ˈspɔːts ˌsentə(r)/
team   /tiːm/
Thailand   /ˈtaɪlænd/
training   /ˈtreɪnɪŋ/
watch DVDs   /ˌwɒtʃ ˌdiː ˌviː ˈdiːz/

4 D Mickey, Millie and Mut

always   /ˈɔːlweɪz/
because   /bɪˈkɒz, bɪˈkəz/
catch   /kætʃ/
every   /ˈevri/
in brackets   /ˌɪn ˈbrækɪts/
park   /pɑːk/
play sports   /ˌpleɪ ˈspɔːts/
table tennis   /ˈteɪbl ˌtenɪs/
tennis ball   /ˈtenɪs ˌbɔːl/
talk to   /ˈtɔːk ˌtuː, tə/
visit   /ˈvɪzɪt/
Why not?   /ˌwaɪ ˈnɒt/

Culture

Canada   /ˈkænədə/
do athletics   /ˌduː æθˈletɪks/
each week   /ˈiːtʃ ˌwiːk/
event   /ɪˈvent/
How often … ?   /ˈhaʊ ˌɒfn, ˌɒftən/
normally   /ˈnɔːməli/
popular   /ˈpɒpjələ(r)/
prize   /praɪz/
race   /reɪs/
sports day   /ˈspɔːts ˌdeɪ/
summer   /ˈsʌmə(r)/
winter   /ˈwɪntə(r)/

Sports

American football   /əˌmerɪkən ˈfʊtbɔːl/
athletics   /æθˈletɪks/
baseball   /ˈbeɪsbɔːl/
basketball   /ˈbɑːskɪtbɔːl/
cricket   /ˈkrɪkɪt/
golf   /ɡɒlf/
high jump   /ˈhaɪ ˌdʒʌmp/
javelin   /ˈdʒævlɪn/
long jump   /ˈlɒŋ ˌdʒʌmp/
netball   /ˈnetbɔːl/
rugby   /ˈrʌɡbi/
snooker   /ˈsnuːkə(r)/

English Across the Curriculum

kind   /kaɪnd/
lots of   /ˈlɒtz əv/
mime   /maɪm/

Musical instruments

clarinet   /ˌklærɪˈnet/
double bass   /ˌdʌbl ˈbeɪs/
drums   /drʌmz/
electric guitar   /ɪˌlektrɪk ɡɪˈtɑː(r)/
flute   /fluːt/
harmonica   /hɑːˈmɒnɪkə/
harp   /hɑːp/
keyboards   /ˈkiːbɔːdz/
percussion instrument   /pəˈkʌʃn
   ˌɪnstrəmənt/
saxophone   /ˈsæksəfəʊn/
string instrument   /ˈstrɪŋ ˌɪnstrəmənt/
tambourine   /ˌtæmbəˈriːn/
trombone   /trɒmˈbəʊn/
trumpet   /ˈtrʌmpɪt/
wind instrument   /ˈwɪnd ˌɪnstrəmənt/
xylophone   /ˈzaɪləfəʊn/

Revision

by car   /ˌbaɪ ˈkɑː(r)/
in the evening   /ˌɪn ði ˈiːvnɪŋ/
turn   /tɜːn/

Your Project

add   /æd/
all week   /ˌɔːl ˈwiːk/
at all   /ət ˈɔːl/
check   /tʃek/
comment   /ˈkɒment/
cycling   /ˈsaɪklɪŋ/
digital   /ˈdɪdʒɪtl/
each other   /ˌiːtʃ ˈʌðə(r)/
every week   /ˌevri ˈwiːk/
face   /feɪs/
guess   /ɡes/
help   /help/
hobby   /ˈhɒbi/
It's time for …   /ˌɪts ˌtaɪm fə(r) ˈ…/
stamp   /stæmp/
take a photo   /ˌteɪk ə ˈfəʊtəʊ/
until (till)   /ənˈtɪl (tɪl)/

5 Places

5 A My room

bedside table   /ˌbedsaɪd ˈteɪbl/
bookshelf   /ˈbʊkʃelf/
carpet   /ˈkɑːpɪt/
chest of drawers   /ˌtʃest əv ˈdrɔːz/
football boots   /ˈfʊtbɔːl ˌbuːts/
lamp   /læmp/
mirror   /ˈmɪrə(r)/
position   /pəˈzɪʃn/
robot   /ˈrəʊbɒt/
rug   /rʌɡ/
see   /siː/
sports star   /ˈspɔːts ˌstɑː(r)/
wall   /wɔːl/
wardrobe   /ˈwɔːdrəʊb/

Prepositions

behind   /bɪˈhaɪnd/
in front of   /ˌɪn ˈfrʌnt əv/
opposite   /ˈɒpəzɪt/
under   /ˈʌndə(r)/

5 B Our house

eat   /iːt/
flat   /flæt/
here   /hɪə(r)/
telephone   /ˈtelɪfəʊn/
to let   /tə ˈlet/

Places

bathroom   /ˈbɑːθruːm/
cellar   /ˈselə(r)/
dining room   /ˈdaɪnɪŋ ˌruːm/
downstairs   /daʊnˈsteəz/
garage   /ˈɡærɑːʒ, -rɑːdʒ/
hall   /hɔːl/
stairs   /steəz/
toilet   /ˈtɔɪlət/
upstairs   /ʌpˈsteəz/

Furniture

armchair   /ˈɑːmtʃeə(r)/
bath   /bɑːθ/
cooker   /ˈkʊkə(r)/
cupboard   /ˈkʌbəd/
curtain   /ˈkɜːtn/
fridge   /frɪdʒ/
light   /laɪt/
sink   /sɪŋk/
sofa   /ˈsəʊfə/
washbasin   /ˈwɒʃbeɪsn/

5 C Our town

Are there ... ? /ˌɑː ˌðeə(r) '.../
closed /kləʊzd/
dream town /'driːm ˌtaʊn/
How many ... are there? /'haʊ ˌmeni '...
   ˌɑː ˌðeə/
I see. /ˌaɪ 'siː/
Is there ... ? /ˌɪz ˌðeə(r) '.../
mention /'menʃn/
town centre /ˌtaʊn 'sentə(r)/

Places in a town

bank /bæŋk/
bus station /'bʌs ˌsteɪʃn/
bus stop /'bʌs ˌstɒp/
café /'kæfeɪ/
church /tʃɜːtʃ/
cinema /'sɪnəmə/
hospital /'hɒspɪtl/
hotel /həʊ'tel/
museum /mjuˈziːəm/
post office /'pəʊst ˌɒfɪs/
shop /ʃɒp/
shopping centre /'ʃɒpɪŋ ˌsentə(r)/
sports shop /'spɔːts ˌʃɒp/
square /skweə(r)/
station /'steɪʃn/
supermarket /'suːpəmɑːkɪt/
sweet shop /'swiːt ˌʃɒp/
swimming pool /'swɪmɪŋ ˌpuːl/
theatre /'θɪətə(r)/
train station /'treɪn ˌsteɪʃn/

5 D Mickey, Millie and Mut

any more /ˌeni 'mɔː(r)/
can (v) /kæn, kən/
carry /'kæri/
cross /krɒs/
day out /ˌdeɪ 'aʊt/
dream /driːm/
feet /fiːt/
fly /flaɪ/
go back /ˌgəʊ 'bæk/
heavy /'hevi/
hurt /hɜːt/
join /dʒɔɪn/
Look. /lʊk/
lost /lɒst/
miss a turn /ˌmɪs ə 'tɜːn/
ride a bike /ˌraɪd ə 'baɪk/
ride a horse /ˌraɪd ə 'hɔːs/
run /rʌn/
ski /skiː/
speak /spiːk/
stop /stɒp/
swim /swɪm/
tired /'taɪəd/
train /treɪn/
We're lost. /ˌwɪə 'lɒst/
wind (n) /wɪnd/
wrong /rɒŋ/

Culture

also /'ɔːlsəʊ/
anything /'eniθɪŋ/
called /kɔːld/
castle /'kɑːsl/
coast /kəʊst/
every day /ˌevri 'deɪ/
famous for /'feɪməs ˌfɔː(r), fə(r)/
good for /'gʊd ˌfɔː(r), fə(r)/
ice rink /'aɪs ˌrɪŋk/
ice skating /'aɪs ˌskeɪtɪŋ/
idea /aɪ'dɪə/

kilometre /'kɪləmiːtə(r), kɪ'lɒmɪtə(r)/
library /'laɪbrəri/
live (v) /lɪv/
market /'mɑːkɪt/
modern /'mɒdn/
near /nɪə(r)/
office /'ɒfɪs/
part /pɑːt/
police station /pə'liːs ˌsteɪʃn/
restaurant /'restrɒnt/
south-east /ˌsaʊθ 'iːst/
think /θɪŋk/
Town Hall /ˌtaʊn 'hɔːl/
visitor /'vɪzɪtə(r)/
water /'wɔːtə(r)/

English Across the Curriculum

any /'eni/
attack /ə'tæk/
bridge /brɪdʒ/
Budapest /buːdə'pest/
buy /baɪ/
by boat /ˌbaɪ 'bəʊt/
Cambridge /'keɪmbrɪdʒ/
cow /kaʊ/
crossroads /'krɒsrəʊdz/
drink /drɪŋk/
easy /'iːzi/
factory /'fæktri/
farm /fɑːm/
flood /flʌd/
ford /fɔːd/
hill /hɪl/
important /ɪm'pɔːtnt/
lake /leɪk/
need /niːd/
Oxford /'ɒksfəd/
Prague /prɑːg/
problem /'prɒbləm/
reason /'riːzn/
safe /seɪf/
sell /sel/
similar /'sɪmələ(r)/
travel /'trævl/
village /'vɪlɪdʒ/
wash /wɒʃ/

Revision

German /'dʒɜːmən/
left /left/

Your Project

bookshop /'bʊkʃɒp/
clothes shop /'kləʊðz ˌʃɒp/
doctor's /'dɒktəz/
fire station /'faɪə ˌsteɪʃn/
get /get/
in the middle of /ˌɪn ðə 'mɪdl əv/
love /lʌv/
take a look /ˌteɪk ə 'lʊk/
walk around /ˌwɔːk ə'raʊnd/
welcome /'welkəm/

6 People

6 A My friends

description /dɪ'skrɪpʃn/
page /peɪdʒ/
quite /kwaɪt/
strange /streɪndʒ/

Physical appearance

bald /bɔːld/
beard /bɪəd/

black hair /'blæk ˌheə(r)/
blue eyes /'bluː ˌaɪz/
brown eyes /'braʊn ˌaɪz/
brown hair /'braʊn ˌheə(r)/
dark hair /'dɑːk ˌheə(r)/
fair hair /'feə ˌheə(r)/
fat /fæt/
green eyes /'griːn ˌaɪz/
long hair /'lɒŋ ˌheə(r)/
moustache /mə'stɑːʃ/
slim /slɪm/
short hair /'ʃɔːt ˌheə(r)/
tall /tɔːl/

6 B Saturday morning

balloon /bə'luːn/
Can I help you? /ˌkæn, kən ˌaɪ 'help ˌjuː/
cup of coffee /ˌkʌp əv 'kɒfi/
department store /dɪ'pɑːtmənt ˌstɔː(r)/
get in /ˌget 'ɪn/
Here they are. /'hɪə ˌðeɪ ˌɑː/
Here you are. /'hɪə ˌjuː ˌɑː/
How much is / are ... ? /'haʊ ˌmʌtʃ ˌɪz, ə
   '.../
ill /ɪl/
in the car /ˌɪn ðə 'kɑː(r)/
lie /laɪ/
Look out of the window. /ˌlʊk ˌaʊt əv ðə
   'wɪndəʊ/
newspaper /'njuːzpeɪpə(r)/
phone /fəʊn/
sit /sɪt/
wait for /'weɪt ˌfɔː(r), fə(r)/
What are you doing? /ˌwɒt ə ˌjuː 'duːɪŋ/

6 C Are we going to the shops?

at the moment /ət ðə 'məʊmənt/
best /best/
brush /brʌʃ/
clothes /kləʊðz/
Come on. /ˌkʌm 'ɒn/
cook /kʊk/
first /fɜːst/
go out /ˌgəʊ 'aʊt/
have a bath /ˌhæv ə 'bɑːθ/
It's raining. /ˌɪts 'reɪnɪŋ/
It's sunny. /ˌɪts 'sʌni/
jeans /dʒiːnz/
on the bus /ˌɒn ðə 'bʌs/
pet show /'pet ˌʃəʊ/
practise /'præktɪs/
smart /smɑːt/
sweatshirt /'swetʃɜːt/
usually /'juːʒuəli/
Well done! /ˌwel 'dʌn/

6 D Clothes

clever /'klevə(r)/
far away /ˌfɑːr ə'weɪ/
gold /gəʊld/
hold /həʊld/
king /kɪŋ/
laugh /lɑːf/
look at /'lʊk ˌæt, ət/
magic /'mædʒɪk/
Majesty /'mædʒəsti/
one day /'wʌn ˌdeɪ/
palace /'pælɪs/
royal /'rɔɪəl/
shout /ʃaʊt/
sing /sɪŋ/
stupid /'stjuːpɪd/
tailor /'teɪlə(r)/
true /truː/

Clothes

boots /buːts/
dress /dres/
hat /hæt/
jacket /ˈdʒækɪt/
shirt /ʃɜːt/
shorts /ʃɔːts/
skirt /skɜːt/
socks /sɒks/
tie /taɪ/
trainers /ˈtreɪnəz/
trousers /ˈtraʊzəz/

Culture

African /ˈæfrɪkən/
(be) born /(ˌbiː) ˈbɔːn/
Birmingham /ˈbɜːmɪŋgəm/
Chinese /tʃaɪˈniːz/
difficult /ˈdɪfɪkəlt/
Edinburgh /ˈedɪnbrə/
English-speaking /ˈɪŋglɪʃ ˌspiːkɪŋ/
European /ˌjʊərəˈpiːən/
Hungary /ˈhʌŋgəri/
Indian /ˈɪndiən/
language /ˈlæŋgwɪdʒ/
learn /lɜːn/
live abroad /ˌlɪv əˈbrɔːd/
luckily /ˈlʌkili/
Manchester /ˈmæntʃestə(r)/
national /ˈnæʃnəl/
New Zealand /ˌnjuː ˈziːlənd/
Nigeria /naɪˈdʒɪəriə/
Scotland /ˈskɒtlənd/
Singapore /sɪŋəˈpɔː(r)/
South Africa /ˌsaʊθ ˈæfrɪkə/
Spanish /ˈspænɪʃ/
Sri Lanka /ˌsriː ˈlæŋkə/
Tamil /ˈtæmɪl/
Turkey /ˈtɜːki/
Turkish /ˈtɜːkɪʃ/
young people /ˈjʌŋ ˌpiːpl/

English Across the Curriculum

closely /ˈkləʊsli/
dot /dɒt/
grass /grɑːs/
hold /ˌhəʊld/
island /ˈaɪlənd/
paint /peɪnt/
painter /ˈpeɪntə(r)/
painting /ˈpeɪntɪŋ/
River Seine /ˌrɪvə ˈseɪn/
row (v) /rəʊ/
stand /stænd/

Revision

late /leɪt/

Your Project

all the time /ˌɔːl ðə ˈtaɪm/
as a rule /ˌæz ə ˈruːl/
banana /bəˈnɑːnə/
corridor /ˈkɒrɪdɔː(r)/
email /ˈiːmeɪl/
feel /fiːl/
fine /faɪn/
keep /kiːp/
look like /ˈlʊk ˌlaɪk/
post /pəʊst/
pyjamas /pəˈdʒɑːməz/
share /ʃeə(r)/
sometimes /ˈsʌmtaɪmz/
upload /ʌpˈləʊd/
website /ˈwebsaɪt/

Vocabulary and Reading

Unit 4

a bit of /ə ˈbɪt əv/
bring /brɪŋ/
cart /kɑːt/
dangerous /ˈdeɪndʒərəs/
dark /dɑːk/
food /fuːd/
go for a walk /ˌgəʊ fər ə ˈwɔːk/
happy /ˈhæpi/
hard /hɑːd/
hide /haɪd/
jump on /ˈdʒʌmp ˌɒn/
loud /laʊd/
noise /ˈnɔɪz/
noisy /ˈnɔɪzi/
quiet /ˈkwaɪət/
soft /sɒft/
story /ˈstɔːri/
suddenly /ˈsʌdnli/
the next day /ðə ˈnekst ˌdeɪ/
Well, ... /wel/
wet /wet/

Unit 5

a long time ago /ə ˌlɒŋ ˌtaɪm əˈgəʊ/
arrive /əˈraɪv/
baby /ˈbeɪbi/
bang on /ˈbæŋ ˌɒn/
bite /baɪt/
bread /bred/
bread roll /ˌbred ˈrəʊl/
cradle /ˈkreɪdl/
cry /kraɪ/
daddy /ˈdædi/
far /fɑː(r)/
fire /ˈfaɪə(r)/
follow /ˈfɒləʊ/
giant /ˈdʒaɪənt/
here comes ... /ˈhɪə ˌkʌmz/
hungry /ˈhʌŋgri/
husband /ˈhʌzbənd/
Ireland /ˈaɪələnd/
land /lænd/
meet /miːt/
Oh dear. /ˈəʊ ˌdɪə(r)/
open /ˈəʊpən/
other /ˈʌðə(r)/
Ow! /aʊ/
pick up /ˌpɪk ˈʌp/
quick /kwɪk/
rock /rɒk/
side /saɪd/
smell /smel/
soon /suːn/
stone /stəʊn/
strong /strɒŋ/
throw /θrəʊ/
What's wrong? /ˌwɒts ˈrɒŋ/
wife /waɪf/
wood /wʊd/

Unit 6

again /əˈgen/
branch /brɑːntʃ/
cheese /tʃiːz/
climb /klaɪm/
crow /krəʊ/
fall /fɔːl/
fox /fɒks/
look up /ˌlʊk ˈʌp/
lovely /ˈlʌvli/
piece /piːs/
please /pliːz/
shine /ʃaɪn/
smile /smaɪl/

OXFORD
UNIVERSITY PRESS

Great Clarendon Street, Oxford, OX2 6DP, United Kingdom

Oxford University Press is a department of the University of Oxford.
It furthers the University's objective of excellence in research, scholarship,
and education by publishing worldwide. Oxford is a registered trade
mark of Oxford University Press in the UK and in certain other countries

ISBN: 978 0 19 476510 7 Workbook
ISBN: 978 0 19 476552 7 Audio CD
ISBN: 978 0 19 476732 3 Access Card
ISBN: 978 0 19 476734 7 Online Practice
ISBN: 978 0 19 476288 5 Pack

Printed and bound in China

This book is printed on paper from certified and well-managed sources

ACKNOWLEDGEMENTS

*The authors and publishers are very grateful to all the teachers who have offered their
comments and suggestions which have been invaluable in the development of Project
Fourth edition. We would particularly like to mention those who helped by writing
reports on Project:*

Slovenia: Jezerka Beškovnik, Lidija Apat

Croatia: Lidija Branilović, Ivana Sauha, Ela Ivanić, Ana Pavić

Czech Republic: Jana Pecháčková, Petra Gušlová, Jana Ferancová, Šárka
Karpíšková, Marie Holečková

Slovakia: Mgr. Zuzana Laszlóová, Mgr. Bronislava Gulánová, Mgr. Peter Humay,
Ing. Zuzana Lennerová, Mgr. Katarina Tóth Mikócziová

Hungary: Judit J. Tóth, Szilvia Csanády, Csilla Papné Szalay, Melinda Bollog

Serbia: Sonja Preda Foljan, Ljiljana Ćuzović

Cover artwork by: Paul Daviz

The publisher would like to thank the following for permission to reproduce photographs:
Alamy Images pp39 (playing piano/RayArt Graphics), 62 (dog/Life on White),
62 (rucksack/Hadrian Kubasiewicz); Corbis pp13 (girl smiling/Kentaroo
Tryman/Johner Images), 35 (twins/Helen King), 57 (resort pool/Richard T.
Nowitz), 62 (watch/Dieter Heinemann/Westend61); Getty Images pp31
(playing flute/Elyse Lewin/Photographer's Choice), 45 (Boy with headphones/
Sri Maiava Rusden); OUP pp2 (Andy/Gareth Boden), 2 (Carla/Gareth Boden),
2 (Joe/Gareth Boden), 2 (Mel/Gareth Boden), 2 (Molly/Gareth Boden), 2 (Ravi/
Gareth Boden), 62 (notebook/Dennis Kitchen Studio, Inc.), 62 (iPhone/Jason
Brindel Commercial), 62 (pencil/Mark Mason); SuperStock p37 (boy on couch/
Tetra Images).

Illustrations by: Piers Baker pp8, 11, 17, 19, 25, 29, 33, 37, 42, 44, 45, 50, 52, 56,
59, 62, 64, 70; Paul Daviz p2 (ex 2); Mark Draisey pp2 (ex 1), 5, 14, 16, 20, 24 (ex
4), 27, 34, 48, 54, 58; Chris Pavely p12 (ex 1); Mark Ruffle pp6, 10, 12 (ex 2), 22,
24 (ex 2), 28, 32, 55 (ex 4 & 6), 57, 61, 69; Simon Rumble/Beehive pp3, 15, 18,
30, 36, 43, 46, 49, 51, 60, 63; Chuck Whelon/Beehive pp4, 9, 23, 26, 38, 41, 53,
55 (ex 1).